MW00412022

Osceola's Revenge
The Phenomena of
Indian Casinos

Brick Tower Press
Habent Sua Fata Libelli

Brick Tower Press
Manhanset House
Shelter Island, New York 11965-342
Tel: 212-427-7139
bricktower@aol.com • www.BrickTowerPress.com

Library of Congress Cataloging-in-Publication Data

Green, Gary.
Osceola's Revenge, The Phenomena of Indian Casinos
Business — 1st ed.
p. cm.

1. Business & Economics / Nonprofit Organizations & Charities / Finance & Accounting. 2. History : Native American. 3. Biography & Autobiography : Native Americans I. Green, Gary
I. Title.
978-1-899694-72-3, Hardcover
Copyright © 2017 by Gary Green
First Edition, July 2017

Osceola's Revenge
The Phenomena of
Indian Casinos

By Gary Green

Table of Contents

Acknowledgments & Dedication

Special thanks to Publisher John T. Colby Jr. of J Boylston & Company, whose vision and support took my desire to share this untold story and turned it into a book.

I want to thank uber-agent Alan Morell, CEO of Creative Management Partners, for his leadership, mentoring, advice, and guidance taking control of my "all over the place" energy and guiding me into this book, a television series, and directions that I never knew I nor my brand could take.

I owe a special thank you to my friend Buddy J. Levy, President & CEO of Gary Green Gaming Inc. (www.GaryGreenGaming.com) and a true visionary pioneer of Indian gaming, long before it was profitable or popular for white lawyer-guys from Texas.

I owe a huge debt of gratitude to Max Osceola of the Seminole Tribe of Florida, one of the true fathers of Indian Gaming, without whom this book and all of modern Indian gaming could have never existed in the form it is today. Max will go down in history along with his ancestor as one of the greatest Native leaders of all time. It is a true honor to know him.

Special thanks to my friend Ernie Stevens Jr, a member of the Oneida Nation and who, as the Chairman of the National Indian Gaming Association, has led a consolidated fight for sovereign rights and bringing Indian gaming to the forefront of the gaming industry. For more than 15 years I have learned much from Chairman Stevens' counselling and leadership.

I thank Chief Harold Hatcher and his Waccamaw Indian People of South Carolina who literally have adopted me into their Tribe as an "honorary" member and shared with me their history, struggles, and glorious culture.

Finally, I dedicate this book to all Native American men, women, children, and their ancestors whose land, culture, and very existences have been and continually are under the most brutal assaults. I thank you for five-decades of welcoming me into your sovereign lands and breaking bread with me, despite the atrocities committed by my people. I thank Pontiac, Tecumseh, Crazy Horse, Chief Joseph, Geronimo, and ... Osceola.

To all I bid: *Shonabish. Miigwetch. Néá'eshe. Sgi. Urako. Pidamaya yedo. Kwakwhá. Hy'shqe siam. Oneowe. Mvto. Akvsv'mkv. Ahéhee'. Qe'ci'yew'yew'. We'-a-hnon. Thank you.*

— Gary Green, Boca Raton Florida 2017

Chapter One

Bugsy Died for Your Sins

*When asked by an anthropologist what the Indians called America
before the white men came, an Indian said simply "Ours."*
—Vine Deloria Jr.,
author of Custer Died for Your Sins: An Indian Manifesto

Almost a billion dollars in cash was set to be transferred in the next
few minutes. The only thing between the assembled Savile-Row-
tailored British investment bankers and $965 million was one lone
traditionally costumed Indian shaman ritualistically performing an
ancient rain dance. The bankers could almost taste the cash, a twenty-
one-times multiple of their earnings.

With an oversized pill-box-hat looking turban, topped by blue,
brown, orange, black, and white feathers, the medicine man was clad
in a red long-shirt satin tunic with beaded tail, wrist, and shoulder
work and topped off with what one the bankers believed to be a Rolex
Presidential wrist watch on a beaded band on his left arm. Here in
Manhattan, the undisputed button-down business center of the
universe, he danced, chanted, and shook mysterious-looking rattles,
not exactly a typical mergers and acquisitions meeting.

While the bankers uneasily shifted in their chairs, several stared
blankly at the holy man's unusual headdress made from colorful wool
shawls wrapped about three-inches thick and tied into seven concentric
bands. Their eyes were almost glazed over as they feigned interest and
understanding of the meaning of the shaking rattles, the chants, and
the strange language of blessing 3.7 billion "kan-cat-ka-hum-kin" being
paid for the worldwide chain of Hard Rock Café restaurants.

For 49-year-old Ian Burke, chairman of the Rank Group, this was
about nothing more than unloading the last of the failed movie
company's incompatible assets. He had already gotten rid of most of

1

their ill-fated leisure businesses: *Butlin's, Warner Holidays, Odeon Cinemas, Pinewood Studios* (home of the James Bond movies, Superman, The Dark Knight, The Hobbit, and hundreds of other films), and the "pub" chain *Tom Cobleigh*. Burke's new focus was to become the leading gaming company in the United Kingdom, Spain, Belgium, and Malta; the iconic but sagging-profit hippy restaurant chain was not a good match for the portfolio of the next gambling empire. It was, at least ironic that the purchaser he had found was a gambling empire in South Florida.

For the Seminole Tribe of Florida, historically one of the poorest Indian Tribes in America, this was the impossible dream coming true. Less than a generation earlier, tribal members were picking oranges with migrant workers for forty cents per 90-pound box. Other tribal members, like Chief James Billie, were earning less than $10,000 a year guiding white northern tourists through "Everglades Swamp Tours"; in fact, it was on one of these tours that an alligator bit off one of Chief Billie's fingers. For Tribal Council Member Max Osceola, this was nothing less than the revenge of his great-great grandfather: the legendary warrior, Osceola, who had died in a Federal prison after being captured in the "Seminole Uprising" 150 years earlier. Max later told me that, for him, it was the fulfillment of his ancestors' vision and the shaman was for public relations to celebrate that fulfillment.

For Hard Rock International, this was a new chapter in rock-and-roll free enterprise. Founded in London in 1971 by the 22-year-old son of the owner of the Morton's Steakhouse chain and his best friend, a wealthy Tennessee expat living in London, Hard Rock had become an icon touting "Love all, Serve all." With more than 7,000 employees, 132 restaurants in 45 countries, seven hotels, and two concert venues, the company also owned the world's largest collection or rock-and-roll memorabilia. In 1990 the founders sold to Rank, who within five years had lost $400 million on one development and driven the company into a Chapter 11 bankruptcy (which was eventually converted to a Chapter 7, triggering immediate liquidation to pay off creditors).

As soon as the dance ended, all of the Hard Rock assets would belong to The Seminole Tribe of Florida—a sovereign nation within the borders of the "Sunshine State" and the only tribe to have never signed a treaty with the United States. Within the tribe's historical context, the medicine man's ritual was more than press release theatrics or superstition; it was a reckoning.

Purportedly a $965 million cash transaction, in reality the Tribe financed the December 2006 deal through both equity from the Tribe and through debt issued by their new operating company, which would control Hard Rock; a pretty sophisticated instrument structure for anyone. As Max Osceola told the New York Times, "Our ancestors sold Manhattan for trinkets. We're going to buy Manhattan back, one burger at a time." Ten years later, Max, a master of one-liners, was still amused at his carefully crafted quip.

Even more interestingly, this near-billion-dollar purchase didn't cut into maintaining the Tribe's fleet of aircraft (and replacing the flagship Gulfstream IV-SP corporate jet formerly owned by Jordan's King Hussein and repainted with Seminole colors), nor did it impact the $120,000 a year dividend checks paid to each of the 3,000+ tribal members (including infants). It did not touch the benefit funds for free health care or free college tuition. Despite the seeming opulence of all that, Max unapologetically reports that this fulfillment of his ancestors' vision took his people from having only one high-school graduate in the 1950s to paid college or trade school for all in the 21st century.

To Burke's team it was a cash deal that would be official as soon as the incessant chanting ended and the documents were signed. To the Hard Rock operators it meant a fresh new life and a real growth track rather than just trying to stay afloat. To the Seminole Tribe, it was the most radical repositioning since they chased Andrew Jackson out of Florida. To the American people, it was confirmation that Indian Gaming had officially become a financial force to be taken very seriously.

By 2017, every person in the continental United States lived within a 90-minute drive of a casino, mostly Indian casinos. Today there are 479 Indian casinos generating almost $50 billion a year in net profits, more than four times what Las Vegas casinos generate. One average-sized Indian casino I operated in southern California routinely generated $100 million a month in gross revenue. These casinos are owned by 244 tribes, less than one-half of the eligible Indian Tribes in the United States. The largest casino in the world, with almost 8,000 slot machines, is an Oklahoma Indian casino located one mile from the Texas border. Yet the industry is still in its infancy and likely to grow even more.

That is where I come in. Every year I am approached by at least a half-dozen of those 321 remaining eligible tribes eager to create their first casino and follow the model created by the Seminole. Typically, I meet with another 10 or 15 tribes seeking to have their land declared legally qualified for a casino; of those eligible tribes, almost all of them have access to some land that is not casino-eligible. In addition to the 565 eligible tribes, there are another 700 (at least) groups who have genetic, historical, and cultural claims to be an Indian Tribe but who are not officially "recognized" by the Bureau of Indian Affairs or who have been "decertified" as Indians by the Department of Interior. (Even the Seminole Tribe of Florida was once a victim of proposed decertification—an attempt thwarted by Max convincing the government to give him 25 years to make the Tribe independent.)

One might think that financing one of these glitter-palace resorts would be a "no brainer," especially in light of amazing success stories like the Seminole, the Poarch Creek, the Chickasaw, and others; but there are legal impediments that actually make it a very difficult transaction. Federal law prohibits mortgage, security interest, or collateral of Indian real estate or improvements, that makes loans almost impossible to guarantee. Outside of the casino world, that particular law also means that the local bank can't even hold a mortgage on a home built on Indian land and cars can't be repossessed for nonpayment if they are parked on tribal land.

Early in the 2000s I took over operation of an Indian casino in Oklahoma where, in lieu of actual financing, a slot machine company had provided the Tribe with three "free" doublewide trailer homes to serve as a casino. In exchange, the company was to be paid 60% of the revenue of the slot machines, leaving the Tribe only 40% for overhead and operations which cost about 49% of the revenue. I immediately canceled the money-losing contract and the slot machine company sent us notice of their plans to repossess their trailers (and hence destroy the casino building). I sharply reminded them of Federal law that prohibited them from repossessing anything on Indian land.

To this day the owner of that company will not do business with me or even say hello when I speak; and the casino trailers are still there.

Another Federal law limits the amount of profit a non-Indian developer can make on the enterprises. A third Federal law requires the investor to provide a source-of-funds trail that prohibits even most commercial banks from qualifying to finance an Indian casino.

Even though Wells Fargo, Bank of America, Key Bank, and other major financial institutions operate Indian Gaming finance divisions, the process at best is precarious even for the most sophisticated financiers. For a decade, the largest financing source was a complex hybrid of a regulated bank and unregulated investment company. This group syndicated financing of more Indian casinos than any other source, but the complexity of the transactions brought scrutiny from Federal regulators who closed the company down in 2010. Unrelated to that, lobbyist Jack Abramoff served four years in Federal prison for conspiring to bilk Indian casinos out of $85 million while ostensibly protecting their rights to have and expand their gambling businesses. One of my former employers, real estate and casino mogul turned U.S. President Donald Trump's one foray into Indian Gaming resulted in Trump being "fired" by the Tribe for what they deemed to be excessive fees. Financing Indian casinos is a treacherous paradigm, even for business sophisticates.

Of the scores of investors who regularly come to me eager to "own a casino," less than one percent are still at the table after they understand the legal dynamics of deal structure for an Indian casino. Of the few remaining, even a smaller percentage are still eligible after I explain the scrutiny their finances and personal lives will have to endure to qualify for the investment.

"The most difficult thing about financing Indian casinos is the complexity of dealing with sovereignty," a Cherokee and Sioux investment banker told me over dinner one night in Las Vegas.

Complicating the investment process almost beyond reasonable comprehension, each of those eligible tribes is recognized by the United States as a sovereign nation. A visit to an Indian casino is not unlike visiting Canada or Mexico except the border crossing is easier.

"We are self-governing sovereign nations pursuant to treaties with the United States," emphasizes my friend Scott Vele, a Mohican from Wisconsin and the Executive Director of the Midwest Association of

Sovereign Tribes. Having dedicated the last dozen years of his life to protecting the sovereign rights of the 35 tribal nations he represents in Minnesota, Wisconsin, Iowa, and Michigan, Vele is not just mouthing rhetoric, that self-determination sovereignty is the very cornerstone of how those 479 casinos can exist.

The laws within those sovereign Indian nations are often in sharp contrast to the laws of the state that surrounds the Tribe. For example, the "Bible Belt" State of Alabama (which has conducted fierce raids against illegal gambling) is totally helpless to regulate the three casinos owned by the Poarch Creek Indians of Alabama one of the most financially successful casino operators in the country. In Florida, when supermodel Anna Nicole Smith died at the Seminole Hard Rock Hotel, the Fort Lauderdale police could not come to investigate and the Broward County ambulance service could not take her to the hospital; those tasks were in the hands of the Seminole Tribal police. On Shawnee land in Oklahoma, murder is punishable by "up to" 12 months in the tribal jail. Unless a Tribe has specifically waived sovereign immunity, even slip-and-fall accidents in the casino can be litigated only in Tribal Court or directly by the Tribal Chief. Even in ferociously anti-casino Texas, lawmakers are completely powerless against the 2,786 slot machines operated by the Kickapoo Traditional Tribe in the border town of Eagle Pass.

Between sovereignty and regulatory controls, financing Indian casinos is only a sidebar to the complexities that allow the very existence of Indian casinos and the billions of dollars they generate. The real challenges are layered within a labyrinth of federal and tribal regulations for management, operation, types of games, employment requirements, payout standards, liability, and use of profits from these palaces. The profits have attracted some of the biggest names in commercial casino operations: Trump, Steve Wynn, MGM, Stations, Lakes, and Caesar's Palace/Harrah's. The complexities they encountered have driven away many of these operators.

These complexities that have kept out many traditional investors and publically traded operators, and investment banks have forced a myriad of "creative" financing schemes, "consulting" agreements, and cottage industries of flimflammers, charlatans, and sharks who make 19th century reservation liquor and gun runners look like saints. That continued history of white exploitation of Native Americans and abuse of their lands has perpetuated centuries-old distrust of white men bringing bags of beads and trinkets. The white debate over terminology of "Indian" versus "Native American" versus "Native" is completely irrelevant in the face of the very basic sovereign struggles against the exploiters.

These are some of the challenges I deal with almost every day. In the storied history of American casinos, the gambling houses within sovereign tribal nations are paragons of regulatory controls, unexpected wealth, and new support industries. Casino gambling is relatively young as a legitimate business. For decades, the only legal casinos in the country were in Nevada and even there it was illegal for a corporation to own a casino until 1968. That year, Howard Hughes forced a change in the state law so that he could buy the Desert Inn after he refused to move out of their penthouse in Las Vegas. New Jersey legalized casinos in 1976 but the first one did not open until 1978. Other states did not follow until the 1990s.

Indian casinos began with Max Osceola's Seminole Tribe in a quasi-friendly legal dance with the High Scheriff of Broward County Florida, and a landmark U.S. Supreme Court case that affirmed tribal sovereignty over state and local regulations. It was not until 1986 that the U.S. Congress acted on that ruling and not until 1988 that it became "legal" for Tribes to begin building casinos.

After the Las Vegas murder of casino pioneer Bugsy Siegel, the mobster Meyer Lansky famously said of his casino empire, "we're going to be bigger than U.S. Steel." In 2014 revenue for U.S. Steel was $17 billion, about one-third of Indian Gaming revenue. U.S. Steel had 42,000 employees, about one-tenth of Indian Gaming's 400,000 jobs. In 2014 U.S. Steel paid no federal tax; Indian casinos paid $7 billion federal and $2.5 billion in state taxes. Meyer was right, and perhaps Bugsy died for those sins. No matter how one analyzes the history of casinos, Indian Gaming is a phenomenon that no one can ignore.

Lamenting the complexities of white involvement in funding and operating Native gaming, I whined one of my latest challenges of "barriers to entry" to a tribal leader in New Mexico. "That's YOUR problem dude; casinos are just coming to life for our people: Bugsy died for your sins," he answered.

Chapter Two

Sovereign Nations Within the USA

It has been said that something as small as the flutter of a butterfly's wing can ultimately cause a typhoon halfway around the world.
—Edward Lorenz,
mathematician, meteorologist, pioneer of Chaos Theory

If a county tax collector in rural north-central Minnesota had not tried to evict an Indian family from their single-wide trailer home over $147.95 in 1975, today's almost 500 Indian casinos might not exist. Truly, one overzealous tax collection served as the classic chaos theory butterfly effect that became the hurricane of Indian casinos.

Two hundred years of courts and laws interpreting a single line written by the American founding fathers were suddenly redefined by that attempted eviction. Such a seemingly routine incident started the modern judicial wind blowing toward re-recognizing Indian Tribes as independent and sovereign nations; a status established in the U.S. Constitution but systematically marginalized (if not disregarded) for more than 200 years.

In its most raw form, sovereignty is the legal right of people to govern themselves; for their government to determine its own destiny, make laws, collect taxes, and protect the rights and welfare of its citizens. In short, sovereignty is the very thing that drove the American revolt against England. The almost 500 Indian casinos across the country legally exist because of the simple reality of "sovereignty."

Despite centuries of martial, economic, cultural, religious, and social warfare against the natives of this continent, the United States actually *does* recognize Indian Tribes as sovereign entities. Article 1, Section 8, Clause 3 of the Constitution assigns Congress the power to "regulate commerce with foreign Nations, and among the several States, *and with the Indian Tribes.*" By placing Indian Tribes' commerce on the same playing field as "foreign Nations," the revered founding fathers not-so-tacitly acknowledged tribal sovereignty (again, by equating regulation of commerce with Tribes to "foreign" nations).

If there was any perceived ambiguity in this wording, the early U.S. government cleared it up by entering into treaties with Tribes rather than simply regulating them; a process reserved for government-to-government relationships. In fact, America's very first international treaty was to grant the U.S. permission to move troops across the land of the Lenape Tribe to fight King George; the treaty refers to the land as the Lenape *Nation* and establishes a protocol for American soldiers to cross through the Nation to get to the coast. Clearly, from the get-go, Tribes were accepted as sovereign nations within the borders of the states.

Underrating that relationship between Tribes and the American government inevitably has led to monumental failures to understand the nature of Indian Gaming and how, for example, residents of Wetumpka Alabama (with a population of 5,726 non-Indians) claim they "woke up one morning" to find a huge casino with one slot machine for every two residents in their little rural town. This "awakening" was after local anti-gambling activists spent three years claiming that the State of Alabama had outlawed gambling and a casino could not be built there—despite the fact that the site was the sovereign land of the Poarch Creek Tribe.

As recently as 2013, the Alabama Attorney General even got into the act, filing a lawsuit claiming the Tribe's gaming machines were illegal under state law. Of course, a federal judge immediately dismissed the suit as frivolous, but the very fact that a State's Attorney General did not understand sovereignty is indicative of how complex the issue is and has been since the U.S. Constitution was ratified.

Today's Indian casinos are the product of a very-specific progression of changing government policies toward "The Indian Problem." From the early 1800s and continuing into the 20th and 21st centuries, a handful of U.S. Supreme Court decisions, Congressional acts, and Presidential Executive Orders shaped both interpretation and understanding of that relationship between nations. Alabama's

Attorney General, that Minnesota tax collector, Georgia goldmine speculators, President Grant, and scores of other powerful influences have tried to either define or abolish that relationship of sovereign nations, but as the very existence of Indian casinos shows—they failed.

Still, a staple for the first-year curriculum in almost every law school is an 1823 Illinois lawsuit called *Johnson v. McIntosh*. The Supreme Court case affirmed sovereignty by prohibiting American citizens from owning sovereign Indian land. At the same time, and seemingly schizophrenically, the ruling established a divine right of the European-settled new American Government to buy and sell Indian land as it saw fit. As a sort of precursor to Manifest Destiny, the ruling allowed the government to grab sovereign land for expansion but prohibited citizens from it.

Following these mixed signals, the government ability to land-grab from sovereign nations came to a head with the passage of the "Indian Removal Act" and the 1831 *Cherokee Nation v. Georgia* case. Again with dual messages, that case affirmed a momentous attack on sovereignty but with a backhanded limitation, this time on states as well as citizens. Gold had been discovered in the Cherokee Nation near Dahlonega, Georgia, and as part of the prelude to what would become the notorious Trail of Tears march, the state annexed the land from the nation. The Tribe sued but the U.S. Supreme Court refused to hear the case, claiming they had no jurisdiction because an Indian Tribe "is not a foreign State within the meaning of Article III (of the Constitution)." The ruling went on to define the meaning of Article III by describing Tribes as "dependent nations, with a relationship to the United States like that of a *ward to its guardian*." This terminology would shape Indian policy for the next 150 years.

A year later, in *Worcester v. Georgia* the same Supreme Court ruled that the Cherokee Nation was, in fact, sovereign after all. Justice John Marshall wrote that States had no rights to enforce state laws in Indian nations. The same ruling rendered the Indian Removal Act invalid and in violation treaties with the various Indian nations.

That ruling might have cleared the issue for once and all, returning affirmation of the original sovereignty of tribal nations. However, President Andrew Jackson refused to enforce the Worcester ruling and continued the rendered-illegal Indian Removal Act. Jackson's policies sent Federal troops to march 16,543 Cherokee people to Oklahoma—

along with Chickasaw, Choctaw, Muskogee, Creek, and Seminole tribal members. Almost 6,000 Cherokee died on the way, about 30% of the tribe.

Despite Jackson's ignoring the court ruling, the "ward to its guardian" status of the first case stuck. It was widely accepted that only Congress had power over Indian affairs and State laws did not apply within Indian nations. Combining the Jackson guidelines and the congressional power over tribes, by the end of the 1800s the official government strategy focused on elimination of sovereign Indian nations and full assimilation of Indians into the U.S. homogeny.

In a delayed Congressional response to *"Custer's Last Stand* at Little Big Horn" (The Lakota Battle of the Greasy Grass), the notorious 1887 "Dawes Act" was designed to resolve the sovereignty issue once and for all by abolishing Indian nations. Based on the "ward to guardian" relationship, the law abolished most Indian nations. The decimation divided tribal land into 160-acre plots deeded to heads of Indian households. For the next 45 years, the Federal Office of Indian Affairs (later the BIA) systematically abolished sovereign nations.

By the time Franklin Roosevelt took office in 1933, two-thirds of all Indian land had been converted to private ownership. With flagrant and brazen disregard of national treaties between the governments of sovereign nations, most tribal land had been sold to non-Indians in tax auctions (because many of the Indians had no way to pay locally imposed taxes on their new land).

"There is no word for 'tax' in any Indian language. This is a European concept. We didn't understand owning land, much less taxing it," Max Osceola laments, with a genuine pain in his eyes and voice.

At the urging of philanthropist Mable Dodge, Roosevelt appointed a new Indian Affairs Director who not only was a longtime advocate for repealing the Dawes Act but also was a crusader against assimilation. Radical sociologist John Collier, in his new role at the BIA, pushed for legislation to restore sovereign nations, for setting up Roosevelt-model Civilian Conservation Corps public works programs for Native Americans, and for federal acceptance of a cultural pluralism offering many tribal philosophies as models for Euro-American white society.

To appease Roosevelt, the 73rd Congress passed the "Indian Reorganization Act of 1934" which, theoretically, ended the Dawes assimilation policies, curtailed the sale of tribal lands, purchased new lands for tribes, created Collier's proposed "New Deal" type social net for Indians, and returned sovereign rights to the tribes.

Conciliating as that sounds, in reality, Congress had a different vision for "the Indian Problem." Congressional conservatives, bolstered by land speculators and several tribes that felt Collier's paternalism was anti-Indian, tempered the reforms by inserting measures to allow for forced full dissolution of some tribes.

The final version of the law mitigated the Administration's guardian-to-ward endowments with paternal limitations on sovereignty and a provision that would allow termination of sovereign nations that the Bureau of Indian Affairs deemed extinct. For the most part, that extinction was a euphemism for genocide driven by the assimilation polices of the Dawes Act. In 1954, the Department of Interior began the full termination and relocation phase of the act and immediately terminated 61 tribal nations, declaring them extinct (despite thousands of natives who identified themselves with the ancestors' heritages).

"The Government had decided that we needed to be terminated. They knew we weren't extinct but they also knew that they were spending a lot of money helping our people. We were not self-sufficient. It is always about money, one way or another. They wanted to terminate us so they could save all that money. What my ancestors wanted was to be self-sufficient; we got there eventually," Osceola says with a combination of wry sarcasm and still-present animosity.

Moreover, the modified Indian Reorganization Act limited the autonomy normally associated with sovereignty. Various actions of a tribal government needed the approval of the Secretary of the Interior, state criminal laws were enforceable in Indian nations, and a variety of sovereign-limiting state laws were sanctioned.

The bureaucratic steps created by that approval process ultimately facilitated the creation of Indian casinos. Since the 1793 "Second Trade and Intercourse Act," the government had kept an "Indian Agency" on most tribal reservations to serve as the liaison with Tribes; beginning in 1906 "Indian Agents" had been called "Superintendents" of Tribes. Under the Reorganization Act, approval of tribal actions had to be a written document signed by the Superintendent, then submitted to a regional office, then to the BIA national office, and finally to the Secretary of Interior. In relatively short order, the bureaucracy of those steps in approving the most routine (and often boring) tribal actions had become bottlenecks. To free up those paperwork logjams, the Department of Interior gave each Superintendent an assistant (called "Tribal Administrator"), who could sign if the Superintendent was otherwise engaged. Additionally, the department instituted a rule that if a regional office failed to act on a Superintendent's recommendation within 30 days, the action was deemed automatically approved and was routinely signed by the Secretary.

Finally, and perhaps the most bizarre to an outside observer, all sovereign Indian lands were seized by the United States government and "held in trust" by the "guardian" USA "for benefit" of the ward-nation Indians. As a result, Indian nations became, physically, totally owned by the United States and held as either a reservation, pueblo, Rancheria, or a trust. This indignity stripped the nations of their land and reaffirmed the century-old *Worchester v. Georgia* to artificially force the Tribes to be *dependent* sovereign nations. As a final ignominy, Congress granted several states total criminal and civil jurisdiction on tribal lands.

That was still the situation in 1971 when Russell Bryan, a member of the White Earth Band of Ojibwe Chippewa bought a mobile home in Itasca County, Minnesota. Russ, his wife Helen, and their children parked their trailer home on the Reservation. In June of 1972, Itasca County sent the Bryan family a tax bill for $29.85, which a few months later increased $147.95. That was the day the butterfly's wings began to flutter.

The tax collector notified the family that if they failed to pay the bill, eviction and a tax sale of the mobile home would begin. Unable to afford either the tax bill or lawyers, the Bryan family turned to the free Reservation Legal Services Project. Lawyers there filed a class-action suit to halt state and county from collecting taxes from Indians on any tribal land. They lost at District Court and on appeal to the Minnesota Supreme Court, in 1975 the County announced they would move forward with the eviction and tax sale. In a dramatic last minute "Hail Mary pass," the lawyers appealed to the U.S. Supreme Court.

On June 14, 1976, the world changed when the high court issued a unanimous ruling in favor of the Bryan family. Beyond saving the family home, as a class-action case, the ruling had the effect of reaffirming the constitutional sovereignty of tribal nations. This was much more far-reaching than simply clarifying that county personal property taxation does not apply on Indian land; the ruling acknowledged that "general state civil regulatory control over Indian reservations" was unconstitutional. Former U.S. Assistant Secretary for Indian Affairs, Kevin Washburn, summarized the impact as "an erroneous $147 County tax notice helped bring Tribes $200 billion in Indian Gaming revenue."

Secretary Washburn's assessment is not a political overstatement. In 1979, Broward County Florida (Fort Lauderdale) sent a "cease and desist" letter ordering closure of the Seminole Tribe's high stakes bingo hall calling its operation "illegal gambling" under Florida law. In "Seminole Tribe of Florida v. Butterworth," the courts cited the Bryan case and ruled that since bingo was legal in Florida restrictions civil, not criminal, and therefore outside of the state's authority over a sovereign nation. The U.S. Supreme Court opted to not even hear the case, citing that it had already been decided in the Bryan case.

Following the rules, the Seminole Tribe had submitted plans to build their bingo hall to the Department of Interior's local Superintendent, but that Superintendent announced his retirement and was in the midst of a 365-day paid vacation. Written approval, under the anti-bureaucracy provisions, fell to the Seminole Tribal Administrator, a not-yet-thirty-year-old tribal member who had been hired for the job: Max Osceola.

"I asked (Chief) Jim Billie if this would be good for our people. He said it would and I signed it then sent it to Atlanta," Max recalls.

Atlanta was the location of the regional Department of Interior office. "In Atlanta they looked at it as just more paperwork from Florida. A steel Butler building to be a bingo hall, how important could that be? They tossed it into a stack of other papers and forgot about it. Two months later it was automatically approved," Max reminiscences.

"During 'Seminole Tribe of Florida v. Butterworth', they said 'This couldn't have been approved; was it ever signed off on?'" Max laughs as he remembers 1979. "That was in April, and my son was born in December. It was a good year," he adds.

Legal review of the approval document clearly shows the signature of BIA Tribal Administrator Max Osceola. If there is a seminal moment in the creation of the phenomena of Indian casinos, it is in fact a "Seminole moment": the signature of Max Osceola.

Then in 1987, the issue again returned to the U.S. Supreme Court.in "California v. Cabazon and Morongo Band of Mission Indians." The highest court reaffirmed the Bryan ruling by quashing that the State of California's attempt to shut down poker rooms operated by two small tribes in that state. California had argued that poker rooms and high stakes bingo operated by the Cabazon and by the Morongo Band of Cahuilla Mission Indians violated state law. The Supreme Court responded that since California allowed—*and in fact encouraged*—legal gambling with their state lottery and private poker rooms, then gambling was not a criminal act but a regulated one. Regulation is civil and not criminal, therefore the Bryan decision was further defined by ruling that state civil law does not apply in sovereign Indian nations that may be within the state's borders. That ruling affirmed tribal sovereignty over any civil issues; traffic laws, lawsuits, corporate law, licensing, labor law, taxes, or any other issue regulated but not criminalized by states.

Gaming aside, the Bryan decision also laid the foundation for the Seminole Tribe of Florida to begin selling tax-free cigarettes on their reservation. State taxes on tobacco were regulatory; as a sovereign nation, the Seminole Tribe was exempt. Max recalls daily seeing lines of cars miles long on State Road 7/U.S. Highway 441 in Hollywood Florida, all smokers wanting tax-free cigarettes. Tribal self-sufficiency was on the way.

The butterfly wings set in motion by that county tax collector helped reaffirm more than 500 independent sovereign nations within U.S. borders, nations exempt from State civil law.

Chapter Three

A Deliberate Radical Transformation

We must kill the Indian to save the man.
—Lieutenant Richard Pratt,
1879, Founder and Superintendent of Carlisle Indian School

Tuscarora Nation Chief Howard Brooks pulled me aside to warn, "My brother, be careful; things are not always what they seem to be or what he tells you they are. That man will not look into my eyes with truth when he talks with me. I am not even sure he is Indian. You know the FB-Eyes are everywhere. Do you know that he tried to convince me to bomb the post office?"

It was early 1973 and as a 19-year-old folksinger, I was the guest of the Tuscarora nation in Maxton North Carolina. Generally, I was there to discuss the struggle for recognition of decertified tribes and sovereignty-related issues. Specifically, we were meeting to discuss what else we could do on day 42 of the 71-day standoff between U.S. Marshalls and Indian activists on the Pine Ridge Reservation at Wounded Knee South Dakota.

I could not have imagined that these meetings would lead to my involvement in a backroom battle against a Mormon Congressman to create what would become the Indian Gaming Regulatory Act. Legislation that would enable Indian casinos—or, for that matter anything to do with casinos—was the furthest thing from my mind as we strategized support activities for the radical American Indian Movement.

For most of the unwavering Indian leaders who were at the forefront of the struggle for self-sufficiency (and who became pioneers of Indian Gaming), these were obscure and seemingly unimportant events; six years before Max Osceola's signature officially launched the Indian casino movement. On the other hand, the United States government, and specifically the FBI, declared that Wounded Knee was "an Indian uprising" with "radical white reinforcements" bent on sedition.

In the early 1970s, the most headline-grabbing advocacy group against the Indian Termination Policies was the Minneapolis-based American Indian Movement (AIM); sort of a Native America version of the radical Black Panther Party. In 1969, an AIM group called "Indians of All Tribes" had seized Alcatraz Island in the San Francisco Bay, citing an 1868 treaty guaranteeing that all abandoned federal lands would be returned to the Natives from which it had been stolen. On Thanksgiving 1970, AIM had seized the "Mayflower II" reproduction of the original ship as it landed in Plymouth. In 1971, AIM activists occupied Mt. Rushmore. In 1972, AIM organized a cross-country caravan from the west coast to the BIA's Washington DC office to call national attention to lost sovereignty. When the Nixon administration canceled previously approved meetings with the cross-country travelers, AIM seized the Bureau of Indian Affairs offices. These and other publicity stunts were created to call attention to treaty violations and repeated encroachments on sovereignty. The organization was widely known as the most high-profile voice among Natives.

A country music folksinger calling Nashville home and attending the University of Tennessee in Knoxville, even at 19 and three years before I had my first record contract, I had been drawn to Native American issues. Indoctrinated by Johnny Cash's *Bitter Tears* album of Indian songs, I started singing Peter La Farge Indian songs, just as Cash had done. That led me to sharing a stage in 1972 with Floyd Red Crow Westerman, a Sisseton Wahpeton Oyate Indian singer-songwriter eighteen years my senior but decades wiser.

Red Crow told me that before he was ten years old he was taken from his family and forced to attend the Wahpeton Indian Boarding School, 70 miles from home and in another state. Forbidden to see his parents, his traditionally long hair was buzz cut American military style. If he was caught speaking his native language, school officials would washout his mouth with burning lye soap. If he dared practice his people's traditional religion, he would be locked in a guardhouse with only bread and water for several days. His painfully tearful recollections combined with the vivid La Farge/Johnny Cash poetry gave me vignettes of American Indian history that I prayed were isolated incidents.

Unfortunately, they were not and that reality fueled my outrage. Beginning in 1869 with President Ulysses Grant's "Peace Policy," the U.S. government launched a network of mandatory boarding schools for Indian children. Forbidding them to speak their languages, wear traditional clothing, or allow boys to have traditional long hair, the stated goal of the schools was to assimilate the Natives to Euro-American standards. This ferocious appropriation of children was often brutal with Native children beaten or otherwise severely punished for the offenses of "acting Indian."

In 2007, Amnesty International reported that "authorities took Native children from their homes and tried to school, and sometimes beat, the Indian out them." There are multiple documented cases of children beaten for practicing their religion, and girls as young as nine-years old raped repeatedly as punishment for not keeping "orderly households." These barbaric schools reached their highest enrollment a hundred years later in the mid-1970s with 60,000 enrolled students, ongoing at the very time I was learning about them. Though the practice of forced enrollment and kidnapping children who evaded the schools ended in the 1930s, as of 2017 there are still almost 5,000 students enrolled in these schools.

Creation of the schools was the first step in that calculated and organized assimilation and annihilation of the race; a second step, launched in 1887, was to decimate the land of the Nations. It was Red Crow's horror stories about the continuing decertification and assimilation that had brought me to organize and sing for Indian causes.

Through a rally and concert I had raised about $10,000 ($53,000 in 21st-century money) for Wounded Knee, and depending on whether one believes me or the FBI, the money was used either to send blankets and soup or to fill a rented truck with automatic rifles and ammunition that I somehow would smuggle into the occupation on day 11 after a 15-mile-zone barricade was relaxed.

The Indian Reorganization Act of 1934 had assured that the BIA would control elections and government appointments in the few tribes remaining after the massive decertifications. By 1972, on South Dakota's Pine Ridge Reservation, tensions between the BIA-supported government and tribal elders were so intense that the elders formed their own competing government through their "Oglala Sioux Civil Rights Organization." The new government demanded impeachment of the BIA-supported government and called in AIM for support. The "recognized" Chief, backed by BIA police officers, created a personal militia that he called "Guardians of the Oglala Nation" and opponents called by the acronym, "GOON". Tensions between the two groups had become violent with assaults on both sides.

The Council of Traditional Chiefs and the matriarchs of the clans voted to gather in the reservation town of Wounded Knee, which historically had been the site of one of the largest massacres of Indians in American history. About 200 people (more than half of them elders, women, and children) moved into the church at Wounded Knee and demanded that the U.S. Government reopen treaty negotiations with the Traditional Chiefs. AIM supporters from all across America headed to the reservation to support the elders and make a stand for sovereignty.

On the heels of significant publicity defeats at the hands of AIM, the United States government responded with an impressive military presence looping a 15-mile barricade around the town. For the first time since the Civil War, US Troops were dispatched in a domestic operation with unprecedented overkill. The 82nd Airborne and the Sixth Army were dispatched to join US Marshals, National Guard from five states, and FBI agents. A full battalion of snipers, supported by daily fly-overs by Air Force F-4 Phantom fighter jets, made a stand against 200 men, women, and children inside a wood-frame church building. To hold back the "Indian uprising," the military brought 17 armored personal carriers, a dozen .50-caliber machine guns, 41,000 rounds of M-40 high explosives for M-79 grenade launches, helicopters, 130,000 rounds of M-16 ammunition, and a procession of helicopters. Seven hours away at Fort Carson, Colorado, an armed assault unit was billeted to 24-hour full alert. The military cut off water, electricity, medical supplies, food supplies, and eventually banned media coverage of the siege.

Despite all the publicity about the siege, in those pre-Internet days I (and probably most Americans) were practically oblivious to just how seriously the U.S. Government was taking a radical demand for Indian sovereignty. Three years later the extent of Federal resistance to that sovereignty confrontation became terrifyingly clear when a

Senate Subcommittee revealed the magnitude of the military response and the depth of covert infiltration of both AIM and of any organization supportive of the sovereignty movement for Tribes.

Opening the hearings, notorious segregationist Senator John Eastland decried AIM as a "subversive" organization with stated treasonous goals of "dissolution of the BIA; establishment of a Free Indian Congress; establishment of Indian sovereignty; trade and economic negotiations with foreign countries, including communists; and the establishment of independent Indian states." Senator Eastland, who previously had notoriously claimed that the 1954 school desegregation ruling had destroyed the US Constitution, gave his committee an opening tying AIM to misguided churches, the Mafia, Fidel Castro, Chairman Mao, the Weather Underground, the Minnesota AFL-CIO, the Soviet Union, the United Electrical and Radio and Machine Workers of America, a new "underground railroad" for smuggling surveilled Indians, and the FDA's Food Stamp program. The senator was especially concerned about the sources of AIM's "mysterious financing" and support from white American "radicals."

Despite these fanatic rants from the committee chairman, testimony did reveal a far-reaching network of undercover agents embedded in key AIM positions and within support organizations. According to testimony: paid FBI infiltrators established and opened the AIM national office in St. Paul Minnesota; AIM leader Dennis Banks' personal bodyguard was an embedded agent; AIM's security director and various AIM regional office spokesmen were either FBI agents or paid moles; and various non-Indian support groups and fundraising organizations were assigned fulltime, taxpayer-financed, undercover agents.

The US Government was very serious about opposing sovereignty. Later, congressional and judicial hearings revealed that beyond the small army of implanted agents, the FBI's COINTELPRO program added a series of forged documents, perjured depositions, break-ins, illegal wiretaps, fabricated evidence, and at least two attempted murders of AIM leaders. As one Federal Judge put it "the FBI had stooped so low as to pollute the waters of justice." U.S. Senator James Abourez stormed out of Eastland's hearing, denouncing it as attempting to justify some of the darkest days of FBI abuses and open war on Indian sovereignty.

The time was the radical early 1970s, and like Senator Abourez, the American public's reaction was more supportive of the Indians than of the military reaction. Popular objection reached its height when at the Academy Awards ceremony, Marlon Brando refused to accept the best actor award for "The Godfather" and instead sent Native American actress Sacheen Littlefeather to protest the government presence at Wounded Knee. That controversy triggered an entire movement of "cultural workers" (actors, artists, musicians, and writers) joining in support of AIM.

It was in that atmosphere that I organized the largest political rally that the University of Tennessee had seen; 25,000 people—more than 10% of the population of the entire county. With myself serving as the musical opening act and master of ceremonies, I invited speakers from the nearby Eastern Band of Cherokee Indians in North Carolina, from the local Unitarian Church, from the Anti-Defamation League of B'nai B'rith, from the university's anthropology department, celebrated civil rights activists Carl and Anne Braden, and a representative from AIM. Although AIM didn't have sufficient notice to send a speaker, the Cherokee speaker had been to Wounded Knee with two other Cherokee members, one of whom was killed by an FBI sniper a week before our rally. With free admission, I structured the rally like an old southern rival meeting, passing my cowboy hat (and Kentucky Fried Chicken buckets) for donations that added up to a little more than $10,000.

Documents, later released under the Freedom of Information Act, revealed that my fundraising garnered the attention of the anti-Indian hysteria. Heavily redacted FBI documents show that conversations between University Police and federal agents pondered over how the money would be used, despite its religious origins. FBI Special Agents began questioning my friends and professors, trying to determine if I had been to South Dakota and if I had attempted to buy firearms or buy food.

Unaware, unconscious, oblivious, and riding on the success of the rally, I formed TAIMSG, Tennessee American Indian Movement Support Group, with two other volunteers. The two religious groups provided office space and the anthropology department provided staff. We began a southern circulation of the radical New York Indian newspaper, *Akwesasne Notes* and launched a speakers' bureau to talk about sovereignty issues and tribal termination. Two weeks later the B'nai B'rith Executive Director called to tell me the AIM representative had finally arrived.

It was a full month before Chief Brooks' ominous warning, and it would have never occurred to me that my guitar-playing support of tribal sovereignty would warrant having my very own personal government agent assigned to report on my activities. Eventually I suspected, and later confirmed on my own, that the man identified at various times as John Bright Star, John Britestar, John Two Owls, John Bear Bow, and Indian John was not an Indian. The government hearings and the FOIA documents confirmed that he indeed was part of that Nixon-era COINTELPRO program to "infiltrate" the American Indian Movement and destroy calls for sovereignty. Chief Books had been absolutely correct in his suspicions.

From the moment I met John Bright Star there were enough red flags that a more experienced organizer would have reacted; but for me, it was all just benign to a teenage country singer. I arrived at the TAIMSG office to see a very tall man wearing a leather cowboy hat with a single eagle feather in it. He had long coal-black hair tied into two pigtails, and deeply reddened skin. He wore a red sort-of-tunic shirt with a thunderbird silkscreened on the back and some intricate beadwork around the wings of the bird. He was adorned with what appeared to be several thousand dollars' worth of silver and turquoise jewelry. He wore faded jeans with a medicine bag tied at the waist just above the watch pocket. On his feet were beaded leather moccasins.

For all the world, he looked like he had just stepped out of a "Buck Loner" western. Costuming aside, it was his first words that should have sent me to the door; he actually began by saying *How* and raising his right hand in Jay-Silverheels-Tonto style. Seriously, and it got worse.

He continued, actually uttering, "White men have spoken with forked tongues to my people for many-many moons. I come to you today from a mighty war party ready to fight back for Native American rights that white fathers have stolen. AIM is that war party."

I hid my face to keep from laughing at this parody and he continued to talk, less in stereotype caricature and more in the political rhetoric of the day. It was so absurd that I wrote down his words verbatim and still had those notes 40 years later. Highly suspicious, I promised to get back to him in the next 48 hours.

Back at home, I called Western Union and sent telegrams to Red Crow, Carl Braden, the AIM national headquarters, and Vernon Bellecourt (brother of the co-founder of AIM). All responded that they knew John, and in fact, he was a representative of AIM, former president of the Chicago chapter, and even a national council member. Only my old friend Red Crow Westerman expressed any doubt; he said that he did not know John very well and that John acted "flakey" but he came with good credentials.

Based on those recommendations, I gave John the organizational reigns of TAIMSG and another almost $10,000 we had raised for operating expenses. In 21st-century money, that is more than $100,000 between the two rounds. In hindsight, it is no wonder that my activities raised official eyebrows.

Working the phone, I put John on every television news show, radio interview, newspaper, and college campus in the state. Yet when I tried to discuss sovereignty with him, he wanted to talk about marijuana distribution rather than Indian issues. He had a scheme to double the TAIMSG money by buying marijuana and reselling it at double what he would pay for it. I wanted no part of that; still, I ignored the warning signs and tried to focus on tribal issues and more specifically on poverty. He even accompanied me to the meeting with Chief Brooks, or, more accurately, I accompanied him.

A couple of months into his stay, John brought in a woman who he introduced as his wife. She and her five children (from previous marriages) moved into a cabin on 200 acres, about 20 miles away; a cabin apparently donated to John by a deputy sheriff in the next county. The cabin had no doors, no insulation, well-pumped water, and no electricity. John also managed to have a large ten-year-old station wagon mysteriously donated for his use.

About once every two weeks, he would fly to St. Paul, Atlanta, Charlotte, Chicago, New York, or South Dakota (where, allegedly, he would spend a week in the sweat lodge of the Lakota medicine man, Leonard Crowdog). Each trip he would take the car keys with him and leave the family with no food, heating fuel, money, or transportation. Hence, maintenance and support of the Bright Star family became the daily responsibility of TAIMSG. Less than a political support group, we became a de facto social services agency with a client family.

About a week after the meeting with Chief Brooks, I made one of the food-delivery visits to the cabin. This time we found John's wife, an Indian-looking former Chicago stripper, bruised and obviously beaten. She told us that John often beat her and the children and she could not take it anymore. In her rage she blurted to us, "We aren't even married and he is not really an Indian anyway."

After some calming and then chiding, we convinced her to elaborate on that outburst. She told us that John was a white man from East Knoxville and his mother still lived there. She added that he had been "playing Indian" for about five years and had fooled the leadership of AIM as well. I insisted that she take us to meet the mother.

In a two-bedroom, wood-frame house I met a nice, typically southern, white woman who introduced herself and confirmed she was John's mother. As she talked, I noticed a photo of John on the mantle, short hair, lighter skin, and a U.S. Airforce dress uniform. She told me that she did not know why John had started pretending to be an Indian, but she thought it was when he started working for the FBI after returning from England for Military Intelligence (which he had served for 20 years). The mother assured me that both she and John's late father were white. When I refused to believe that John could be white, she left the room and returned with his birth certificate and an album of childhood photos. The certificate said he was white. She agreed to let me borrow and photocopy the documentation if, in turn, I would agree to get mental help for her son, who she believed was suffering from a mental illness that made him think he was Indian.

That afternoon I telephoned the AIM national office, Carl Braden, and the Anti-Defamation League Director. I then called Chief Brooks in North Carolina to tell him that he had been correct about John. I heard a deep sigh and then he said, "You are welcome in my home anytime." He said nothing else and hung up the phone.

A week later John returned to Tennessee accompanied by a gnarling wolf-looking dog and four FBI agents. He pointed to the dog and said to me, "Do you see that dog? If you feed him, he will be the best friend you ever have; but if you don't feed him and then beat him, he will kill you and eat you. You have beaten me and refused to feed me. You have destroyed everything." He turned and left. I never saw him again until the congressional hearing. His wife and children moved to

Arizona. We closed the TAIMSG office, humiliated to have been duped. If the goal had been to discredit our work, it was fulfilled.

By the time, amendments to the Freedom of Information Act allowed release of the files on the incident I was working as a newspaper reporter for a mid-sized daily newspaper. The last entry in the highly redacted file reported that FBI field agents had requested to do an in-person interview with me but the Director's office in Washington DC refused to approve the request, citing that because I was a member of "the working press" it could possibly be detrimental to "the program." I could only speculate what "program" the memo cited.

As a newspaper journalist and folksinger I continued my work for tribal sovereignty, collaborating most frequently with William Kunstler, who was my personal attorney, a close friend, and renowned for representing the Chicago Seven, the Catonsville Nine, the Black Panther Party, the Weather Underground Organization, the Attica Prison rioters, along with the American Indian Movement. Beginning in the late 1970s. "Battling Bill" (as I usually called him) began telling me about several court cases addressing the sovereignty issue including a fireworks-for-sale case on Alaskan Indian land, a bingo hall case from the Oneida Tribe in Wisconsin, and a 1978 casino case on the Puyallup reservation in Tacoma Washington (United States V. Farris). Battling Bill believed that these cases could eventually open the door for financial independence of Tribes through fireworks, gambling, marijuana sales, prostitution, and other enterprises banned in most states but open for truly sovereign nations.

I contacted Chief Brooks about the prospect and offered to introduce him to Kunstler, but as leader of a non-recognized "splinter-group" Tribe, he was not excited by that vision. Besides, he was embroiled in his own issues. Chief Brooks' people were the descendants of the survivors of the early 18th-century war between his Algonquian people (the "Croatan") and North Carolina settlers thought to be the Virginia Dare "Lost Colony of Roanoke." For decades, Chief Brooks' Tribe had been in a battle with other North Carolina Indians (the Lumbee, the New Croatan, the Cherokee, and an amalgamated group called the "Eastern Carolina Indians") over recognition, sovereignty, and opposition to sending children to Indian schools. The more pressing issues for him, though, were various criminal charges against him stemming from demonstrations, visits from AIM officials, the visit from me, and a host of typical anti-activist charges.

Since I was without a "test case" Tribe, Battling Bill directed my attention to some nonpolitical clients he represented who had financial interests in the new Atlantic City New Jersey casinos. Working closely with those investors, I began looking more closely at the economic freedom that casinos would offer Tribes if the sovereignty issue could be settled. By this time, the Seminole and Cabazon cases had begun and Congress was starting to look at the issue.

Mo Udall, Chairman of the House Committee on Interior and Insular Affairs set the tone, introducing a bill with testimony citing, "Federal courts, and at least two circuits, have determined that, under certain circumstances, Indian Tribes may engage in or may license and regulate gambling activities on the reservations free of State licensure and regulations. H. R. 4566 does not make legal anything that is not already legal under those court decisions. The purpose of the bill is to provide some minimum Federal standards and some protection for Tribes who are otherwise engaged in legal gambling activities."

Udall's generally pro-sovereignty and Tribal supportive bill was countered by conservative Mormon Church director and Ronald Reagan pal, Congressman Norm Shumway from the San Francisco Bay area. Shumway introduced his own bill, announcing, "Indian communities have taken unfair advantage of the unique jurisdictional status of their reservations by establishing large-scale gambling operations. The Indian nations' unique position in the federal system has made the Indians a separate, unaccountable segment of society who claim many rights but deny accountability for commensurate responsibilities." To stir popular concern about Indian Gaming, he and Congressman James Bilbray of Nevada also warned that "the unsavory forces of organized crime" would be attracted to casinos in Indian Country; an amusing assertion coming from a Democrat representing Las Vegas.

Brought to popular support by Wounded Knee, Marlon Brando, and huge pro-Indian rallies in conservative hotbeds like the University of Tennessee, widespread white awareness of tribal sovereignty had been shaped by the 1960s and 1970s radical transformations. Anti-Indian rhetoric had much less impact by the mid-1980s than it would have had a generation earlier in the popular era of Senator Eastland, the Ku Klux Klan, and hate groups.

Many tribal leaders lobbied for, explained, and spoke on behalf of the economic development that would be afforded by casinos and the financial support of health care, education, tribal governmental programs, and a host of basic living benefits. Their passionate and tireless lobbying and support-building left the backdoors open for the non-Indians who had come to understand sovereignty from the organized radicalization of the previous decade.

Those of us who squeezed through that backdoor focused on concentrated opposition to Shumway and the other anti-Indian forces that our Native friends could not. My own role was to defeat Shumway's bill on every level possible; mostly though concerts, writing, speeches, and organizing for his political opponents in elections.

Even then, 210 years after the founding of the United States, we were still dealing with elected officials who were baffled by what they were calling "The Indian Problem"; a very old term. Forty years before the Declaration of Independence, the issue was already being called "The Indian Problem"; a phrase coined in 1735 by French explorer Louis Armand, whose book, *New Voyages to North America* was generally supportive of Native culture, especially Howard Brook's Algonquian ancestors, during the author's travels with Iroquois people. Despite 18th-century zeitgeist terms like "savage generals" and paternal comparisons of Native religions to Christianity, Armand's book actually attempted to lay a foundation for peaceful coexistence on the continent between distinct Indians nations and European invading settlers.

From then even into the 21st century, the core issue of sovereign nations within the borders of the United States is widely misunderstood or out-and-out feared like it was during the AIM era. Beyond relatively benign opposition to gambling, the real issue of sovereign relationships is still inflammatory to all sides when otherwise well-meaning journalists, elected officials, lawyers, and educators whip up centuries-old anti-Indian fervor in attempts to clarify "The Indian Problem."

That is exactly what happened in 2016 when a somewhat respected Indian rights lawyer, after testifying before a Congressional subcommittee on Federal acknowledgment of Indian Tribes, wrote a 400-page supposed exposé explaining that Indian casinos were "invented" through a conspiracy between the Mafia, "fake" Indians, a hapless U.S. Congress, and bribed city government officials. The uproar from that tabloid sensationalism was a whisper compared to the reaction following an earlier *Time Magazine* "special report" assembled by two Pulitzer-winning reporters who argued that Indian Gaming was "created" by Washington as a cut-rate way to move Indians from the welfare system to generating income.

Their article's assertion that the casinos produced an elite class of rich Indians while the majority of tribal members remained impoverished fueled general anti-Indian tirades from wildly divergent fronts. At one extreme citing the article, libertarian columnist William Safire proclaimed that the poorest Indians were getting poorer at the expense of non-Indians hiring lobbyists to create a "Tribal front" for the sole purpose of buying land to build casinos for white men. On the other extreme, responding to the sovereignty issue, the American Family Association warned its 180,000 members that "superstition, savagery, and sexual immorality morally disqualify Native Americans from sovereign control of American soil."

Ernie Stevens Jr., Chairman of the National Indian Gaming Association and a member of the Oneida Nation of Wisconsin, responded with disgust to the *Time* article in an open letter proclaiming that the "story is based on the false and offensive premise that 'Washington' created Indian Gaming as a 'cheap' way to wean Tribes from government handouts."

He continued, "Indian Gaming is not a federal program. Instead, it is one tool that tribes use to generate revenue for their communities. The Federal programs that you refer to as handouts represent an attempt by the federal government to live up to thousands of treaty obligations incurred when establishing the land base for this Nation. American Indians have been victimized by federal policies supporting genocide and assimilation, which took millions of lives and millions of acres of Indian land, and caused economic and cultural destruction. Our grandfathers, Pontiac, Tecumseh, Crazy Horse, Chief Joseph, Geronimo, and so many others, fought for our rights—especially our right to self-government on our own land. The U.S. Constitution, the

President, Congress, and the United States Supreme Court all recognize Indian Tribes as governments."

Pointing to both morality and federal law, Chairman Stevens added, "Tribes use gaming first and foremost for Tribal government programs, community infrastructure, charity, and aid to local governments. Where Indian Tribes have suffered the highest teen suicide rates in the country, Indian Gaming has built schools, funded colleges scholarships, and given our children hope for a brighter future. The Mille Lacs Band of Ojibwe, for example, built two schools and their high school graduates are now fluent in both Ojibwe and English. Where our people suffer epidemic problems of diabetes, heart, and liver disease, Indian Gaming is building health clinics, dialysis centers, and fitness centers."

Chairman Steven's passionate and accurate tirade calls to that central issue of Tribes as sovereign nations within the boundaries of the United States. Despite the rational and irrational emotional divide, constitutionally proclaimed sovereignty would seem to be cut-and-dried. Unfortunately, it is not... even today.

Chapter Four

Accidentally Opening the Door

Political necessities sometime turn out to be political mistakes.
—George Bernard Shaw

I was waging a musical and publicity war against what I saw as anti-Indian politicians; the two small Cahuilla Tribes in California (the Cabazon and Morongo Bands of Mission Indians) were exploring revenue from cardrooms and bingo halls; and Max Osceola was fulfilling his ancestors' vision. Meanwhile, a tall, young, basketball-playing, Texas lawyer was starting an adventure that would trigger Federal legislation acknowledging the legitimacy of Indian casinos and at the same time putting limits on them. Ultimately, that basketball-scholarship lawyer was destined to be recognized, arguably, as one of the fathers of Indian Gaming.

Buddy Levy was a first-year legal associate at a large Houston law firm with no thoughts, ambitions, nor designs on casinos or Indian Tribes. As with most freshman associates, Buddy handled routine corporate affairs for some of the prestigious firms' less-than-major clients. One of those subordinate clients was a new want-to-be energy company formed by a Houston architect and two fertilizer company magnates from Connecticut.

Pan American Corporation was created to take advantage of the 1970s energy crisis and Carter-era legislation that was predicted to radically alter the oil industry more than anything since the Standard Oil breakup in 1911. Like adoption of the metric system, acceptance of New Coke, a Milli Vanilli greatest hits album, and other great predictions of the era, American consumers' abandoning gasoline didn't happen either. Nonetheless, Buddy's job was to handle all documents, regulatory forms, and negotiations for the new company and its foray into the world of "gasohol"; a technology that had attracted backers as diverse as Willie Nelson and Texaco Oil. Buddy's

30

client's vision was to take the investment frenzy into Indian country in 1978.

The new technology of blending gasoline with at least 10% ethyl alcohol was widely anticipated to be the "killer app" to solve the era's energy crisis. Ethyl alcohol is "drinking" alcohol made by the yeast fermentation of sugar. Beginning in 1976 the government was providing low-cost loans and investment tax credits to the new gasohol industry and massive subsidies to corn growers for their fructose corn syrup; Republican Senator Bob Dole's 1978 Energy Tax Act went a step further and waived the Federal gasoline tax for gasohol. Within the next few months, 25 states also waived their fuel taxes on gasohol.

Inspired entrepreneurs could enter the business with virtually no investment, a government backed low-interest loan, and almost make money before selling the first barrel of the new fuel. The only barrier to entry seemed to be finding an adequate supply of government subsidized corn or cane for the fermentation process. Buddy's clients saw a seemingly unlimited supply of sugar cane for the process on the Seminole Tribe's 82,000-square-mile Big Cypress Reservation in South Florida. They reasoned that if they partnered with the Tribe, they would not even have to buy the sugar for the process. Buddy and his clients negotiated the deal and at the same time struck up a close friendship with Chief James Billie, Max Osceola, and other tribal leaders.

Investing several million dollars into the project and into the economically depressed Tribe, Buddy's team excitedly dedicated themselves fulltime to the project. On January 21, 1981—the first day of the Reagan administration—Carter's "windfall profits tax" on the recently deregulated oil industry became the first casualty of the former president's failed energy program; the gasohol subsidy became the second. So ended the alternate fuel dreams of Pan American Corporation.

Chief James Billie and Max Osceola from the Tribe, and Pan American Corporation's CEO Jim Clare and lawyer Buddy Levy had all become close friends as well as business associates. Though their business relationship seemed to be coming to an end, the bond of friendship between the two white men and the Indians remained strong. A harbinger of most good Indian and white relationships for many years to come, that friendship bond was stronger than written contracts, treaties, or any documents Buddy's quite-formidable legal mind could conjure. Forty years later, Max or Buddy still would drop most anything else they were doing to have lunch or dinner together at a simple phone call from the other.

At the time, the Seminole Tribe still was struggling to find a viable economic development program; the canceled gasohol business had been a promising hope. The fledgling bingo hall in Hollywood Florida was making a little money—enough to pay off the construction loan in six months; but most of the revenue was being gobbled up by white operators (who were under investigation by a Pennsylvania organized crime strike force). Still, Chief Billie believed in the future of Tribal gambling springing from bingo, especially in light of the victory in the Butterworth cease-and-desist case.

Chief Billie recalls constant harassment from Broward County Sheriff Bob Butterworth, beginning the day the bingo hall opened. The Tribe's Washington DC-based law firm told him that the Tribe could not operate a bingo hall at all; and the Sheriff's department argued that the entire enterprise was illegal in Broward County (Fort Lauderdale). Though there were no arrests and no actual enmity, both sides were adamant in their positions.

"There was nothing hostile about it at all; there were no arrests. It was a mutually agreed-on decision to determine the legality of that bingo hall," Buddy Levy explained years later as he described the relationship between Chief Billie and Sheriff Butterworth.

In sharp contrast to the actual SWAT-team like raids and arrests of the Cabazon in Indio California five years later, the Florida challenge was focused on the courts from the very beginning. That made perfect sense given that Butterworth was also a lawyer who would later become Attorney General of Florida and the Tribe (embodied by the contrast between Chief Billie and Max Osceola) was simply seeking viable economic development programs that would free them from being what Billie called "a grant Tribe" of government programs.

Buddy said that the Sheriff and Billie had be sparring over how the courts would view the bingo hall and decided that the simplest way to find out and to tacitly legalize or outlaw the revenue stream would be to test it in a court case. Thus was born the landmark decision and the beginning of Indian Gaming, five years before overzealous California law enforcement decided to raid Indian nations and force the issue to the U.S. Supreme Court.

Riding his belief in the model, Chief Billie began looking for locations to open a second bingo hall; one operated free of the corruption he was feeling at the original location. Though the Tribe had strong historical claim to lands all over Florida, obtaining that land and getting it into government trust was a different matter. Disney had locked up most desirable land in a band across central Florida (all around the Orlando area) and the price of buying coastal land was absurdly prohibitive (especially for a financially struggling Indian Tribe).

As soon as the gasohol project failed, the Chief began eying land in both Tampa, on Florida's west coast, and in Tallahassee, the state capital located in the panhandle of the state. One particularly desirable location, literally in downtown Tampa just off Interstate 4, had been the site of a number of hopeful development projects that had all failed to find funding. Despite the unsuccessful developments, the price of the 8.5 acres remained far beyond the ability of the Seminole Tribe and the land remained vacant. Finally, in 1980, the frustrated City of Tampa government approved the site for a multistory parking garage and began excavating to build a foundation. Part way through the excavating, workers found Indian remains; the site was an old Seminole burial ground.

Despite a mandatory halt to the construction and the inability to use the land for any development purposes, the City remained firm on their pricing of the land, still beyond the Tribe's means. The location was perfect and the population of Tampa was mostly Midwestern retirees with disposable income—the demographic model of bingo players. Not to be discouraged by typical Florida land speculation, Chief James Billie turned to his friends at Pan American Corporation.

Without hesitation and with Buddy's encouragement but the objections of his partners, Jim Clare committed his company to the $1.2 million need to acquire the land and build the hall. Chief Billie, Max Osceola, and the Tribal Council made a deal with the Department of Interior to abandon Tallahassee and have the Tampa land proclaimed Indian trust land. Buddy went to work on the agreement between the Tribe and the company, which included a management contract for Pan American to run the bingo hall.

"I just made it up," Buddy modestly recalls his creation of a business model that would become the template for Indian casinos. "This was uncharted territory. There was no federal jurisdiction and there were no regulations."

It was a time that a traditional loan to an Indian Tribe was a near impossibility. The Bryan/Itasca acknowledgment of at least civil sovereignty had also scared many lenders who realized that they could not secure loans with real estate or other property on Indian land. Despite later solutions and even waivers of sovereignty for certain actions, that realization and bank skittishness continues today; as recently as 2016, I had a respected amusement finance group balk because the proposed project was on Indian land. It is because of that kind of reluctance from traditional finance sources that Buddy Levy created a prototype that could work for all parties.

"We were all friends and had the same goal. Never once did the Tribe not do what they said they would do and never once did we give them any reason to be concerned," he explained, showing the strength of the personal relationships.

Rather than a traditional bank-style loan, Buddy fashioned a business model that would meet the needs of both parties: the Tribe and Pan American Corp. The model revolved around Pan American providing funds for development and operations (the traditional "loan purpose"); and rather than the Tribe offering security interest, they would give Pan American a management operational contract. Buddy wrote a 20-year contract (12 years with the option to renew for eight more) with management fees of 40% of net revenue of the business. As Levy later noted, it indeed was uncharted territory; no one had ever created such a business model.

Since the Butterworth case was still pending in court, the Tribe and Pan American Corp. elected to not open a bingo hall until it was resolved; they did not want to risk the ire of a federal judge. Instead, they opened a smoke shop and an Indian museum and bided their time. When the case was finally decided by a written decision from Judge Lewis Morgan for the majority of the Fifth Circuit U.S. Court of Appeals, the Tribe okayed moving forward with the bingo hall. The business was so profitable and so well managed that Pan American Corporation's investment was fully repaid in the first four months of operation.

Eventually that parking-garage-turned-bingo-hall became the sixth largest casino in the world and the third most profitable. Though Clare's partners left the project early on, seeing it as some sort of "Seward's Folly," Pan American operated the casino from 1980 until 2000; the full 20 years of Buddy's contract.

More importantly, the model of funding and then managing from a vacant lot to a highly successful casino set the bar for the beginnings of Indian casinos across the country. Buddy, who by now had left the Houston law firm and had become part of Pan American, went on to apply the Clare-Levy template to fund and operate the Immokalee Casino for the Seminole, the Sycuan Casino in San Diego County California, the Little Six Casino in Prior Lake Minnesota, Barona Casino in Lakeside California, and a half-dozen other casinos in California and the Midwest.

Widely accepted as the economic development model for Tribal gaming, the Clare-Levy template was duplicated or emulated all over the country. In 1986, Chinese Malaysian billionaire Lim Goh Tong, founder of Genting Gaming, used the model to fund the Mashantucket Pequot Tribe's Foxwoods casino, which would become, for a time, the largest in the world. As recently as 2004, computer guru Gordon Graves, Chairman and CEO of Multimedia Games in Austin Texas, used a modification of the model to fund the Oklahoma Chickasaw Tribe's Winstar Casino in exchange for a semi-exclusive placement of his slot machines in the casino; ten years later Winstar has surpassed Foxwoods as the largest casino in the world, with almost 8,000 slot machines (primarily from charging "placement fees" to multiple vendors).

Max Osceola's vision of gaming as an economic development tool became more of a necessity when the Reagan administration began their early 1980s slashing of social programs like Indian Health Service. More than 80 tribes had followed either the Clare-Levy-Seminole model or the Cabazon model and had some form of gaming on their reservations…mostly as a survival tool for tribes.

Anti-Indian and anti-gaming forces began to marshal organized opposition to the tribal enterprises. In Florida, the Disney family-friendly-vacation industry set their sights on stopping the Clare-Levy model. The State of California filed a Seminole-style case against the Barona Tribe, claiming the Butterworth decision was not precedent setting and only applied to Florida. Opponents in New York and Wisconsin rolled out the Nevada Congressman James Bilbray argument of the "danger of mafia infiltration." Even more panic ensued two-and-a-half hours from New York City, when Connecticut's attempt to halt the Foxwoods bingo hall failed to prove the state's contention that the Pequots were not "real" Indians and their land was not a reservation.

On the Federal level, the Reagan Department of Justice proposed legislation to replace sovereignty with strict adherence to state civil and criminal laws on all reservations. The Bureau of Indian Affairs assembled a National Indian Gaming Task Force, made up exclusively of tribal leaders, which recommended that the BIA regulate gaming and thereby codify it as a legal activity. Meanwhile, some members of Congress began pushing the Norm Shumway legislation to curtail gaming by further encroaching on tribal sovereignty to curtail gaming completely.

As early as 1983, Frank Duchenleaux, the Legal Counsel for the House Interior Committee (and a Cheyenne River Sioux Tribal member) drafted legislation for pro-Indian Congressman Mo Udall to introduce. That bill would have affirmed tribal sovereignty over their gaming enterprises and at the same time put limitations on the Clare-Levy model management companies. Labeled the "Indian Gaming Control Act," the wording prohibited "individual Tribal members or nonTribal individuals or entities" from holding "any proprietary interest in Tribal gambling operations or a percentage interest in the gross or net revenues from such operations." In effect, it would have put Pan American out of business and destroyed the primary avenue Tribes had to finance gaming operations. Massive tribal opposition as well as testimony from institutional associations of Tribes killed the bill.

The last-straw driving force seemed to have been the Cabazon case. Seven different Indian Gaming bills were introduced in the next session of Congress, the Seminole and especially Cabazon cases, at their core, had been about the difference between criminal and civil authority, regulation, and enforcement on sovereign Indian land within states. Both of the court decisions had redefined the long-standing doctrine of implicit divestiture in which the extent of tribal sovereignty was paternalistic controlled despite treaties, and that opened a number of potential issues far beyond the operation of bingo halls.

The Florida case had been a Federal Court of Appeals case, but Cabazon had been decided by the U.S. Supreme Court, which very clearly stated: *To the extent that the State seeks to prevent all bingo games on Tribal lands while permitting regulated off-reservation games, the asserted state interest in preventing the infiltration of the Tribal games by organized crime is irrelevant, and the state and county laws are preempted.* That pretty well shut down the leading arguments against the bingo halls and established U.S. policy by judicial review.

Amid the flurry of new Indian Gaming bills came Senate Bill 555 from Senator Daniel Inouye of Hawaii, who headed the Senate Indian Affairs committee. Senator Inouye, who later said that he had sponsored the bill because he was angry over so many attempted encroachments on Indian sovereignty, teamed with Representative Mo Udall of Arizona and with then-Representative John McCain of Arizona to push the bill, which became "Public Law 100-497 An Act to Regulate Gaming on Indian Lands."

As soon as the bill landed on his desk, President Ronald Reagan rushed to sign it into law before George Bush's presidential election 22 days later. The political expediency strategy was that there would be no time for any backlash from the bill until 1989, an "off year" for elections. On October 17 1988, President Reagan signed the bill that became known as the Indian Gaming Regulatory Act (IGRA).

Despite what seemed to be the best of intentions by Senator Inouye, IGRA was controversial from the onset—even in Indian country. Many tribal leaders saw it as a protection of their sovereign right to operate and regulate their own casinos; other tribal leaders saw it as an attack on sovereignty by imposing government regulations on their regulatory authority.

Max Osceola said, "IGRA didn't give us anything; it only took from us."

Buddy Levy, who eventually became in-house counsel for the Seminole Tribe's business committee, agreed with his friend's assessment but added, "What it DID accomplish was that it assured us that no government agency or the State would show up at the door, seize the money, and arrest everyone."

In fact, IGRA did both, as Levy acknowledged. It did mandate federal and state recognition of the legality of Indian Gaming and in doing so protected it from Cabazon-style raids. At the same time, the very fact that a new federal bureaucracy (a statutorily created National Indian Gaming Commission) was administering rules and regulations in sovereign Indian lands was one more example of imperialistic trespassing into the affairs of sovereign Indian nations.

Wendell Chino, the President of the Mescalero Apache Nation and a self-described "red capitalist," was so incensed by IGRA that he and Red Lake Band of Chippewa Chairman Roger Jourdain filed a federal lawsuit to overturn the new law. In the late 1990s, ten years after losing the lawsuit, Chino (who had held office since 1955) told me that he always saw IGRA as a frontal attack on economic sovereignty by allowing states to interfere with the government-to-government relationship between a Tribe and the U.S. federal government.

The BIA's National Indian Gaming Task Force morphed into a trade association for tribal casinos called "National Indian Gaming Association" (NIGA). Buddy Levy's business model survived, albeit now with strict regulations. Max Osceola's grandfathers' vision was about to be fulfilled.

IGRA was a 25-page law; long in the big picture of typical Federal legislation. The accompanying *Title 25 Chapter 29 of the U.S. Code and Part 25 of the Code of Federal Regulations* added another 191 two-column, single-spaced, 8-point-type pages of regulations and bureaucracy to enforce IGRA. The authors of IGRA and their subsequent regulatory zealots had no idea of what kind of paradigm-changing doors they had inadvertently opened.

The butterfly wings of IGRA, set in motion by that Itasca county tax collector, helped re-affirm more than 500 independent sovereign nations within U.S. borders; nations exempt from many State civil laws.

Chapter Five

Bingo? It LOOKS Like a Slot Machine to Me

(Invisible Bingo Cards and Virtual Ping-Pong Balls)

It depends on what your definition of "IS" is.
—President Bill Clinton

From IGRA and its voluminous support regulations came a bizarre combination of a loophole in the legal definition of "bingo," some diabolically clever computer programming, and the lingering cold-war era belief that "if it looks like a duck and quacks like a duck then it must be a duck." Together, these three non-sequiturs allowed sleepy exsiccating bingo halls to metamorphose into a business with revenues five times greater than Microsoft and Google added together.

It is probably important to the Elvis impersonator on the Las Vegas strip that you believe that his performance is just as good as the King of Rock and Roll; he really needs for you to buy into that illusion. I am equally certain that when you purchase a cola drink at the local super-center, it is important to the purveyor of that soda for you to believe it tastes exactly like Coca-Cola or Pepsi. Likewise, when I am running an Indian casino (or when I am leading a slot machine company), it is important to me that you believe that playing your favorite game in Las Vegas is identical to playing the same game on tribal land. All three examples are carefully crafted illusions.

When you play a traditional Vegas three-reel slot machine, there are about 64,000 possible outcomes of each play of a game; that means there are 64,000 possible ways for you to win or lose on each spin of the reels. By comparison, on many Indian casino slot machines there are about 552 septillion possible outcomes, meaning there are 552 x 10^{24} possible ways for you to win or lose on each spin. This does not mean that either machine is fairer than the other is, or that you have a better or worse chance of winning with either counterpart. It *does* mean there is a huge difference in the games, despite my best attempts (as an operator) to convince you they are identical.

Calling them "Las Vegas Style Slot Machines" and using the same game titles, themes, graphics, sounds, cabinets, playing method, and other ornamental cues, Tribes, manufacturers, and casino operators have tried every marketing trick we know to convince players that there is no need to go to Vegas to find their favorite slot machines. Not only are these games not identical, but many times they are not even remotely similar beyond those cosmetics.

The roots of my deception to you are found early on page three of IGRA. Among the terms created for and defined by the Act are three "classes" of games. "Class I" games are defined as ceremonial games historically played by Tribes and having prizes of insignificant value. "Class II" is defined as bingo and similar games, including technological aids to playing the games. Finally, "Class III" games are defined as all other forms of gaming and include slot machines, table games, parimutuel betting, sports books, and any Vegas-style casino games.

The law goes on to delineate regulation and taxation of each class of games. Class I games are solely within the purview of the Tribe. Class II games, when played in states that allow some form of bingo, are regulated by the Tribe with some National Indian Gaming Commission (NIGC) guidelines but no state interference or taxation. Class III games are strictly forbidden except in states where casino gambling is already legal; in those states, a Tribe must enter into a to adhere to state laws, regulations, and taxes on the games and revenue.

Again, IGRA specifically outlaws Las Vegas style slot machines at Indian casinos unless the state government enters into an agreement with the Tribe to allow that kind of gambling. Yet in a state like Alabama, for example, which has banned casinos and vehemently refused to negotiate with the Poarch Creek Band of Indians, three of the Tribe's casinos legally operate almost 6,000 slot machines in the state. That paradox is rooted in a legal magician's slight-of-hand that makes those knock-off colas and the faux-Elvis' look authentic and even desirable.

While Alabama is a great example, because the Poarch Creek's machines are among the most profitable in America, the model is widespread through at least 28 states and rooted in the complex shell game that allowed Indian casinos to exist in the first place. Indeed, the largest casino in the world, the 8,000-machine WinStar World Casino on the Oklahoma Texas border, grew from a loophole in the legal definition of bingo and the technological ability to masquerade that game inside a slot-machine-looking cabinet.

Bingo itself was the invention neither of church fundraisers, carnivals, nor of Indian reservations, though each had a hand in it. The game apparently began in the 16th century with an Italian state-run lottery that featured a ball-draw and some letters printed in columns on a card with numbers under the letters. At least by the early 1900s a version of the game had found its way to the carnival circuit in the USA and was being played in horseshoe-shaped booths filled with numbered cards and small piles of beans.

The carnie would draw a small wooden square from a cigar box, call out a number that was printed on the square, and wait for players to check their cards to see if the number called matched a number on their card. If the number matched, players would place a dried bean on the card over that number. Once a player filled a line of numbers on their card, either horizontally, vertically, or diagonally, they would call out *Bean-o!* (because of the beans they were using to cover the numbers). Winning players would get a doll or some other carnival prize.

The folklore of bingo tells us that in 1929, a traveling salesman named Ed Lowe bought some dried beans, a rubber-stamp numbering kit and some cardboard to start his personal home version of the game. During a bean-o party at his house, one of his players was getting more and more excited as she got close to winning. When she finally won, she jumped from her seat, became tongue tied, and instead of shouting "Beano," she wildly stuttered "B-B-B-BEAN-GO!" There was such excitement and laughter about it all that Lowe decided to market the game and call it "BINGO".

While there probably is *some* truth to that version of the story, let's cynically also consider that "beano" was probably a public domain game (and word associated with the game) and the new "bingo" word was something that could be copyrighted, patented, and sold. We *are* talking about a business, after all.

Regardless of the origin of the name, several months after Lowe's Bingo hit the market as a home party game, the salesman was approached by a priest from Wilkes-Barre, Pennsylvania with an interesting Bingo problem. The priest had bought several sets of Lowe's two-dollar bingo games to use as a fundraiser for his church, but each game produced half a dozen or more winners because of the duplication of winning combinations in each box and then even more duplication because he bought several game sets. Salesman Lowe could immediately see the tremendous market in fundraising with Bingo if he just could work out that little kink of duplicated cards.

At an absurdly high fee (a charge per card of up to $100 near the end), he hired a Columbia University mathematician to devise 6,000 different card combinations for him. Suddenly BINGO was a real business and Lowe was marketing to churches, schools, and civic groups. From there it was a short step to commercial bingo halls and the tremendous popularity of the game.

The game was so simple to play that it became engrained into the American psyche from children's birthday parties to the Catholic Church's sodality. In the 1950s and early 1960s when I was growing up, American Bingo was played with 75 ping-pong balls, each of which was imprinted with a number from 1 to 75. In addition to the number on each ball, there was also a letter on the ball (either B, I, N, G, or O).

Basic bingo has not really changed since those days. A bingo player's card has 25 squares that are arranged in five rows and five columns. Each column is headed with a letter (either B, I, N, G or O) and each square has a number in it. The "B" column has five numbers randomly from the range of 1 to 15; the letter "I" has five numbers from 16 to 30; "N" has only four numbers from 31 to 45 (with the center space on the card in the "N" column as a "free" space); "G" has five numbers in the range of 46 to 60; and "O" also has five numbers taken from the range of 61 to 75.

The 75 ping-pong balls are put in a wire drum or a plastic air-blower and are drawn out one by one. A caller reads the letter and number on each ball. Players look for a matching number on each of their cards and when they get a match of adjacent numbers in a row spelling B-I-N-G-O or get numbers in a row under any letter, they win.

The history of bingo itself plays a vital role in understanding what goes on in tribal casinos. Like thousands of churches, charities, and strip-mall storefronts, many Tribes used bingo games as a fundraising activity. This was Chief Billie's model managed by Pan American and Buddy Levy's contract. By the 1980s, there were so many people traveling to Indian reservations to play bingo that IGRA actually had to define bingo: *the game of chance commonly known as bingo (whether or not electronic, computer, or other technologic aids are used in connection therewith)*. Those 14 qualifying words with their parentheses became the magical IGRA loophole that opened Pandora's box.

In the early 1960s when I first started playing bingo in commercial halls, I paid ten cents for each card per game. Typically, a good player could accurately play four or six cards when a number was called. In those days, we covered the plastic reusable cards with a popcorn kernel (replacing dried beans), but by the early 1970s that had evolved to disposable paper cards marked with an ink blotter called a "dauber" (to "daub" the number on the card). The bingo hall would make about 60 cents per game off me or about six bucks an hour before they deducted the costs of payouts. After payouts, the house would make about $4.50 an hour from my play. Even in the 1960s' dollars (about $34.50 in today's money), it took a lot of players to make bingo profitable. In the Seminole/Levy early bingo halls, masses of players were attracted by gargantuan payouts.

By the late 1980s (when IGRA was written) "electronic daubers" had been invented, allowing Indian casino players to keep track of hundreds of cards at once. Suddenly the cost of playing one game of bingo went up from a dime up to as much as $25 or $30 for a "session" of maybe twelve different games with 100+ cards per game. Proportionally, the chance of winning went up as well...and the length of time between winners went down. The bingo halls made more money. Throw in the vast number of players who showed up for the high-limit payouts (instituted by the Seminole Tribe of Florida), and suddenly bingo halls were more than merely profitable.

With an electronic dauber, a player could rent an electronic unit buying a fixed number of bingo cards for the unit—from one to several hundred. The most common electronic units looked like an oversized calculator, but rather than calculator keys they would have the letters B-I-N-G-O and numbers from 0 to 9. When a bingo number was called, the player would press the keys for that number (*B and 8* for "B-8" or *O and 7 and 2* for "O-72," for example). The electronic unit then would search all the cards loaded into the unit (hundreds possibly) and if any of the cards contained the entered number, the card would be marked or "daubed" automatically. The player did not have to ever look at the cards; the machine did it all. In a sense, it was virtual play. When a unit "won" a bingo, a floor runner would come to the player and visually confirm the winning electronic card to pay the prize or money to the player. All the machines then would be automatically reset for the next game. This was the most advanced "technologic aid" that existed when the parenthetical portions of IGRA were written. Some congressional staffer or research assistant probably thought they were writing an all-encompassing definition of bingo to prepare for the coming technological evolution.

My own introduction to the next technological evolutionary step, and the key to modern Indian casinos, began shortly after the dot-com bubble began in the mid-1990s. I was standing at a booth at a casino trade show looking at an "electronic bingo game" that made my eyes want to jump out of my head. For all the world, this game looked like a slot machine: spinning reels of cherries, bars, and lemons; a one-armed-bandit pull handle; coin and bill slots; and all the cling-clang excitement of any other slot machine. I walked up to the machine, put my coins in, pulled the one-armed-bandit handle, and watched the video-game-looking slot machine reels spin. Bar-Bar-Cherry. No winner. I put another three coins in to spin again. Bar-Bar-Bar. I won!

It was a slot machine! But it was not EVEN a slot machine; it was an electronic dauber on steroids. My putting the coins in the machine triggered a series of computer processes that were totally invisible to me but were happening in a fraction of a second on the computer inside the slot-machine-looking cabinet. Putting the coins in the machine "bought" an *invisible* ("virtual" in computer lingo) bingo card; a card that was only on the computer and running as a program in the background that I could not even see. I am serious: an INVISIBLE bingo card!

Pulling the handle on the slot machine triggered two functions in the invisible computer program. First, it drew invisible (again "virtual") ping-pong bingo balls from an invisible ("virtual") ball hopper. Seriously, follow me here: *we are talking invisible ping-pong balls too*. Then it *automatically* virtually (or invisibly) "daubed" my invisible bingo card for any matching virtual (invisible) numbers. Again, all unseen by me and happening in less than a second.

Pulling the handle also started a video cartoon movie running; which is all I was aware of (and, frankly, didn't know it was just a movie or a cartoon). The "movie" was of three slot machine reels spinning...looking like a real slot machine in Las Vegas, Atlantic City, Reno, or any other "real" casino. I thought I was playing a slot machine, not running a movie of a slot machine. When my invisible bingo card "won," on my second play, the video movie stopped with three bars on the "pay line" so that it looked just like a slot machine.

The salesman explained to me that three bars on the video screen were a "technological aid to bingo." I immediately recognized the parenthetical phrase from IGRA, as he explained that the aid used the movie to show an *invisible* (virtual) diagonal bingo on the virtual (invisible) bingo card. Three cherries would have been an electronic facsimile of a vertical bingo. Three lemons would have been an electronic facsimile of a horizontal bingo. Winning the thousand-dollar top jackpot on the machine would have been with a virtual full-card-cover bingo... on that invisible bingo card, of course.

I couldn't believe that it was bingo; it looked like a slot machine. My immediate thought was, "what a diabolical way to circumvent Federal law for Tribal bingo halls; they could all become casinos!" Here was the progression from failing bingo halls to billion-dollar glitter palace casinos: Bingo halls with Bingo games disguised as slot machines and playing like slot machines.

Initially, when this technology of invisible bingo was first devised, it was widely seen as such a slimy interpretation of loopholes that the major slot machine manufacturers would not have anything to do with it at all. The largest (at the time), respectable, publicly traded slot machine corporations like IGT, Bally, Aristocrat, and the others totally ignored that market, opting to avoid the seeming sleaze of this "gray area" of gambling.

This inventive "technological aid" allowed Indian casinos in states with no casinos to have slot machines—or at least something that looked and acted like slot machines. Suddenly any state that allowed bingo in any form could have a full-fledged tribal casino. It was nothing short of a genius bypass of at least the intent of creating three classes of games; it was a "work-around" to the limiting of sovereignty imposed by IGRA's arbitrary control of Tribal revenue options.

With slot-machine-looking games filling Indian bingo hall casinos, players began to demand their favorite Las Vegas and Atlantic City slot machine titles, themes, and names. The final steps for creating modern Indian casinos began in 1996 with a relatively amazing way to convert familiar slot machines into the virtual bingo format. Sierra Design Group (SDG) was a brilliant little technology company founded by a casino industry veteran who created a way to allow those familiarly branded slot machines to operate as those virtual Bingo devices. The bingo-only Indian "casinos" could use the SDG platform so that players now could play slot machines they recognized from Vegas, Atlantic City, or Tunica casinos.

Using SDG's servers and bingo platform (or video lottery platform in some states), two major breakthroughs were accomplished. First, the favorite branded games were brought to the players in areas where those very games effectively had been outlawed. Much more importantly for the development of the industry was the actual licensing of game programs that IGT, Bally, Aristocrat, and others leased to SDG. This allowed the big companies to see how well their games would perform in the market, without having to risk the investment of converting their titles into the seemingly *phony-baloney* bingo platform. If the SDG experiment was a success, then it would be a positive metric for the big boys to consider entering the market.

It happened fast. Revenue from the pseudo slot machines was unprecedented. Per machine, a typical bingo faux-slot was making the casino five to ten times more money than real slot machines were making casinos on the Las Vegas strip. Seeing the trend, Bally Gaming, the Reno Nevada-based giant, bought Sierra Design Group and instantly was in the Indian casino market. The former owner of the then-third-largest commercial slot machine manufacturer, Aristocrat, joined with Bally's former CEO to found an exclusively Class II slot machine company. Once obscure "gray area" slot machine companies were suddenly legitimate and viable businesses with Class II slot machines.

By 2004, a host of government regulators—and ultimately federal courts—had reaffirmed IGRA's tribal sovereignty for regulating bingo. The platform, the games, and the market were all officially sanctioned as legitimate, legal, and no longer a "gray area" of the law; all the doorways were open and all the roadblocks were cleared for corporate America to enter Indian Gaming. Still, the largest and most successful slot machine company at the time, IGT, would not take the plunge into the world of faux-bingo; and IGT dominated casinos with their "Class III" games making up more than 70% of an average non-Indian casino.

In attempts to convince the slot machine giant to make their iconic games available on the new platform, I made repeated trips to their headquarters in Reno with my CFO, who tried to convince them of the economic benefits of Class II games. We presented financial modeling, market assessments, customer interviews, and emotional arguments to lobby for the games. Even presenting with the Arlo-Guthrie-esque "glossy pictures with circles and arrows and a paragraph on the back of each one," nothing seemed to work. At long last, we found the corporate-world argument that convinced the stodgy industry oligarch to enter Indian country: I, personally, agreed to take the first 600 machines off the Reno assembly line. At long last, they agreed with a guaranteed order that would make their first two years' quota, and six months later I installed the new games in an Oklahoma tribal casino. Class II slot machines were finally accepted industry-wide.

Still, even with the SEC-watched corporations in the market and the biggest of the big games in the casinos, it is hard to forget the foundation of this entire business line: cartoon representations of invisible bingo cards and invisible ping-pong balls. Concerning electronic bingo and facsimiles of bingo, it really is as President Clinton said on another subject: *it depends on what your definition of "IS" is.*

Chapter Six

The New Treaties; State Compacts

No state shall enter into any treaty ... No state shall, without the consent of Congress ... enter into any agreement or compact with another state, or with a foreign power...
— Constitution of the United States,
Article I Section 10

Forty-four states plus the District of Columbia operate government-owned gambling enterprises—lotteries. Nevada and Mississippi don't want the competition to their commercial casinos; Alaska and Hawaii haven't felt competitive pressure from surrounding states (since there are none); and politicians in Alabama and Utah have cited religious objections to gambling. The remaining states are in the gambling business.

Following the economic crisis of 2008, the ten-to-twelve-figure annual revenue of Indian casinos (billions of dollars) seemed very attractive to states struggling with budget deficits; especially states that have already tasted gamblers' cash in their State lotteries. More and more, states began looking for ways to tax or otherwise share that income generated by the sovereign nation gambling enterprises within their borders, enterprises that in most cases compete with the state-owned gambling businesses.

Though it took states a while to understand its value, the Indian Gaming Regulatory Act gave them a path to getting their hands on some portion of those Indian Gaming dollars. In fact, IGRA actually compelled some states to sign compacts with Tribes. The goldmine in those compacts is the ability of the state to negotiate a tax on gambling revenue for Class III games.

In 2015, Max Osceola's Seminole Tribe of Florida presented the state with the largest Class III share for any state ever. The compact proposal offered Florida at least $3 billion over seven years, from $325 million the first year up to $550 million in the seventh year. By way of comparison, California's 73 tribal casinos that same year made about $7 billion per year, the highest in the nation; of that, they paid about $241 million to the state. Tribes in Oklahoma generated $3.8 billion in gaming revenues from 124 casinos and paid the state about $125 million. The Florida compact proposal would cover only the Seminole's seven casinos with Class III casinos, quite a comparison.

IGRA defined "Class III" gaming in a very broad description of: *all forms of gaming that are not Class I gaming or Class II gaming*. It goes on to mandate that Class III gaming is only legal for a Tribe if it is located in a state that already permits such gaming. In 1988, when IGRA was signed into law, only Nevada and New Jersey allowed legal (non-Indian) casinos and no new jurisdictions were anticipated. New Jersey had no recognized tribes; Nevada had 19 recognized tribes but only three were well-organized and none of those three were either in large populated areas, tourist areas, or even easily accessible by public highways. In effect, the inclusion of "Class III" as a definition in IGRA was expected to limit the types of gambling a Tribe could operate: Class I and Class II only.

To further prohibit all games except paper bingo (since electronic Class II games had not been invented yet), the language of IGRA requires that a Tribe wishing to operate Class III games (presumably in one of those two states) is required to request the state *to enter into negotiations for the purpose of entering into a Tribal-State compact governing the conduct of gaming activities*. Then, to balance IGRA's paternal restrictions on sovereignty, the law set a 180-day time frame for completing negotiations; if a state fails to negotiate "in good faith," the Department of Interior will force a binding compact. In the entire history of IGRA, since 1988, the Department never utilized that power; in every case the parties eventually reached agreement.

Together, these provisions make it clear that IGRA was written to restrict the Cabazon, Seminole, and other bingo Tribes from ever expanding beyond their then status quo. So imagine the surprised jolt for Connecticut Governor Bill O'Neill when he received a certified letter demanding Tribal Compact negotiations only five months after IGRA passed. O'Neill's staff assured him that the only governor that should have received such a letter was Bob Miller of Nevada; yet the first IGRA demand to negotiate came in a state that thought they were nongaming.

The Mashantucket Pequot Tribe took the issue to Federal Court, claiming that because Connecticut law allowed charitable organizations to operate "Las Vegas Night" fundraisers, then Class III games were legal in the state and Connecticut was therefore required to negotiate with the Tribe. The state's Attorney General insisted that charity games for "play money" in no way resembled real gambling games for real money. The Tribe countered with the Cabazon and Seminole precedent that if the game is not a criminal activity then the rules and payouts are regulatory/civil and THAT regulation is within the scope of the Tribe's sovereign rights.

Both the U.S. District Court in Hartford and the Second Circuit Court of Appeals agreed with the Tribe. When the state still refused to negotiate, the lower court judge followed the IGRA mandate and ordered mandatory mediation (in this case by a retired Federal Judge). Each side was to submit their own version of a compact and the mediator would decide on one, the other, or portions from each.

With real negotiations looming, both the State of Connecticut and the Pequot Tribe needed gaming regulatory expertise to create what would become the first Indian Gaming compact in U.S. history. Both sides wanted to assure fair, secure, and honest games with a legitimate regulatory structure. Choices for experienced American gaming regulators were limited to Nevada or New Jersey, and clearly Connecticut had more geographic, cultural, and political affinity with New Jersey than with cowboy and organized crime tainted Nevada.

After extensive research into that small universe of gaming regulators, the state had their sights set on New Jersey's former Assistant Attorney General, G. Michael Brown. Already known as a fierce prosecutor of organized crime and widely credited with driving the Genovese Family out of New Jersey, Mickey (as he was known) had been tapped in the late 1970s by New Jersey Governor Brendan Byrne to lead enforcement of New Jersey's new Casino Control Act.

Decades later, former New Jersey Secretary of State, Joan Haberle recalled Mickey as the driving force in shaping her state's well-known tough casino licensing process. "He was the first person to head that department, I think Governor Byrne called him 'Director of Gaming Enforcement', and he was very strict in those investigations," she remembered. "My daughter worked for him for a while—she hated it, but not because of Mickey, bless his heart—he was the best, but that work was very intense and draining," Joan told me in 2016.

"When Mickey left that position, he went back to his law firm. I think they did some work in Australia and for some other casino states in the U.S., then he and Bob (Winter) went to Connecticut," she explained, adding, "And Al (Luciani) went with them too."

Meanwhile, for his research, the lead counsel for the Tribe reached out to the Attorney General of New Jersey, for whom he had interned during law school. Haberle remembered, "there was no question; he immediately recommended Mickey to represent the Tribe. He also recommended Bob Winter and Al Luciani."

Luciani had been a member of Byrne's staff policy group that wrote the New Jersey gaming regulations first casino that was licensed in the state.

"The Indians hired Al as one of the first executives at Foxwoods and he was in charge of all their design and construction and eventually the grand opening up there," Joan explained. "And Bob eventually became the General Counsel for Foxwoods. You know, he was the guy that led the investigation in Pennsylvania at Three Mile Island nuclear disaster and got all those managers fired," she added.

General Counsel Robert T. Winter had been another New Jersey Assistant Attorney General and had formed the state's first Organized Crime Task Force, indicting and convicting more than 200 mobsters. After Foxwoods he went on to become the CEO of the Navajo Nation's gaming projects and created four casinos for them.

But, it was Mickey Brown who the Tribe hired to draft the compact and lead the creation of the first Indian casino regulatory structure under IGRA. No doubt the state was disappointed that the Tribe had hired their first choice for the process, but Brown and his team's reputation was so stellar that the state decided not to hire outside counsel and handle it themselves.

"Mickey was the best. He did everything for them; he brought that whole thing together for them, created it all out of nothing, got the money, and then ran it for them," Haberle added, noting that in 1993 Brown became CEO of Foxwoods.

Joan's sentiments were echoed by long-time casino advertising guru, Frank Palmieri, who was a close friend of Brown's. "Mickey was a bulldog. You know, he is the person who brought in Genting's and Lim Goh Tong's investments that built Foxwoods," he praised. The Genting Group is a Malaysian casino conglomerate with a $24 billion market cap; Tong was its founder.

Brown submitted to the mediator the Tribe's proposed compact, which he wrote modeled on and pulling heavily from the regulations he had written for the State of New Jersey a decade earlier. The State of Connecticut also submitted their proposed compact, which they too had modeled on the New Jersey standards written by Mickey Brown.

Once Mickey realized that the two proposals were near identical, he tactfully withdrew the Tribe's compact proposal completely and agreed to the state's submission of his writing. With only one proposal before him, the mediator ruled the negotiations complete and it appeared that the first Indian Gaming compact in the country was about to become reality.

Still the state refused to sign the agreement, with the Attorney General's office stubbornly arguing that Connecticut was a nongaming state and sanctioning charities' "Las Vegas night" fundraising events was in no way authorizing gambling of any form in the state. Holding out for a ruling from the United States Supreme Court, the A.G.'s office seemed convinced that the entire matter would be moot once the high court overturned the Circuit and Appeals decisions and acknowledged the common sense of the state's position.

Not only did the Supreme Court not jump onboard with Connecticut, but they completely refused to hear arguments for the case, remanding it back to the original Circuit Court decision. Finally, the State was obligated to sign their own negotiated compact.

In relatively short order, the Tribe began construction on Foxwoods Casino, which would eventually become, for a time, the largest casino on the planet with a longtime monopoly on day-trip business from Massachusetts, Rhode Island, Connecticut, Long Island and the northern suburbs of New York City—much easier to get to than Atlantic City (and with a lot less street crime).

As significant as the early victories by the Seminole and the Cabazon and as paradigm changing as the Clare-Levy business model, the Pequot's leverage of Tribal sovereignty was equally game changing. The once impoverished Tribal members had strategically negotiated a sustainable economic development model that would become the template for any Tribe in a state with charitable or any form of casino games.

The Supreme Court's tacit affirmation of the demand-for-compact model changed everything. Suddenly, every state that had charitable Vegas-style game events and a federally recognized Tribe became a contender for full-blown Las Vegas style casinos.

By the time the U.S. map was dotted with forced-compact casinos and those new slot-machine-style electronic Class II bingo machines in multiple states, the economic impact of Tribal gaming finally began to sink in to even the most anti-Indian states. In the Connecticut, the compact had the casino agreeing to pay 25% of their slot revenue to the State of Connecticut. That number would eventually bring a quarter-of-a-billion dollars a year to the state. That is BILLION; of course other states were taking note!

Nonetheless, for a variety of noneconomic reasons, several states still resisted negotiating compacts with Tribes; most notably Florida (the birthplace of Indian Gaming) and Oklahoma (home of more than 100 Indian casinos), among a handful of others. Ostensibly, the act established a procedure for dealing with such resistance. Some of the pro-Indian authors of IGRA had built in a system of checks and balances to assure that Tribes would have some relief if a state obstinately refused to negotiate.

IGRA provided Federal Court jurisdiction for any Tribe that felt a state was not negotiating in "good faith" (or refusing to negotiate altogether). Once a court determined that a state had failed to negotiate in good faith, the federal court could order both parties to reach a compact agreement within 60 days. If they failed to reach agreement in that time frame, the court could order a mediator to review submissions from each side and determine which would be the compact for the Tribe. If the parties had not signed the mediator's selected compact within another 60 days, the Secretary of the U.S.

Department of Interior could impose a compact on the state, which would allow the Tribe to conduct Class III gaming.

Never in the history of IGRA has a Secretary of Interior stepped into the process; it never got that far. The closest it ever came was with the original Foxwoods court-ordered mediator. That is until 1996, when once again Max Osceola's Tribe became the precedent setter, this time not so favorably for Tribes.

In 1994, the Seminole Tribe sued Florida and Governor Lawton Chiles for violating that good-faith-negotiations requirement of IGRA. Lawyers for Florida countered that sovereign immunity applied to the State as well as to the Tribe and that under the 11th Amendment to the U.S. Constitution the State was protected from lawsuits. In a five-to-four 1996 decision, the U.S. Supreme Court ruled that a state's sovereignty protected it and its governor from such lawsuits (despite the long-standing legal doctrine of "Ex parte Young").

The case effectively nullified that provision of IGRA and forced the Department of Interior to rewrite the Code of Federal Regulations to bypass the judicial review to allow appeal of "bad faith" directly to the Secretary of Interior. In subsequent years, several Tribes tried that route and were defeated by court challenges citing the 1996 Seminole ruling.

An alternate Tribal route to a compact has been to put the issue in front of either state legislators or even in front of voters for a statewide referendum. The latter is the route we took in Oklahoma to finally get the country's most tribally populated state to sign a compact. Almost one-third of the Native American Indian population of the United States lives in Oklahoma, and despite compacts in many other states the casinos there were all Class II only.

One minute after midnight on January 1, 2005, Oklahoma Governor Brad Henry and Absentee Shawnee Tribal Governor Ken Blanchard met to sign the first compact in the history of that state. The previous November, about 60% of the voters in Oklahoma had approved a ballot measure, "Question 712," to authorize a prewritten model compact.

I was the CEO of Governor Blanchard's Tribe's gaming enterprise and had appeared on dozens of radio and television shows across the state extolling the benefits of a Tribal compact; not the least of which was a 10% tax on gaming revenue.

As part of the nationally broadcast program, *All Things Considered,* the National Public Radio affiliate in Oklahoma City, KGOU, carried the most in-depth reporting and analysis of the voting season. They featured a long interview with a representative from the horseracing industry in the state, a spokesman for a Baptist Church anti-gambling coalition, and me. My remarks on that show were pretty standard for the speeches I was giving all over the state; rather than play a unifying political role, I elected to take a hard-core "take it or leave" attitude to the voters.

After a particularly fierce tirade from the Baptist on the evils of gambling in general, I lashed back hard. "Here's the deal; here is the bottom line of 712, all nonsense aside: Gaming is not going anywhere. We are making a ton of money. This is the one shot for the citizens of Oklahoma to share some of that money with Indian Tribes," I barked in my best Donald-Trump-esque voice that I had honed from my days as his marketing vice president.

"If it doesn't pass, guess what? My machines aren't going away. I am building a new casino out on Interstate 40 that is going to have 2,500 machines whether 712 passes or not. This is the chance for Oklahoma voters, Oklahoma citizens, to share in the wealth." I continued, threatening to open a large Class II casino that would be beyond the state's control, regulations, or taxes.

Since the tax money generated from a compact in Oklahoma would be statutorily earmarked for education, I made one more slam of brashness toward opponents to the measure, "This blows my mind about Oklahoma: we are number 50 in education; we are the worst in the entire country. And this is our chance to move up on the scale and become part of the 21st century; become part of the United States." My Trump-ean superlatives were in high gear.

Before I began my media tour through the state, the polls indicated that the measure could go either way. Most polls put us winning with about 51% but a margin of error of 3%. The more loudly I ranted on radio and television, the better our numbers got. Finally, on Election Day, November 2, 2004, the measure passed with 849,882 votes to 579,311, roughly 60% of the votes.

The measure enacted the model Tribal Gaming Compact and a provision that once at least four Tribes signed, the three horseracing tracks in the state could also have Class III games. Tribes were happy.

The horseracing industry and "horsemen" were happy. The voters were happy.

The law was to go into effect on January 1; hence Governor Blanchard and Governor Henry meeting at one minute after midnight to sign the compact. On New Year's Day of 2005, I became the first casino operator in Oklahoma to have full Class III games and legal live blackjack tables.

Chapter Seven

The Scams, Renegades, Comancharos, Financing Schemes, and Con Men

I don't feel we did wrong in taking this great country away from Indians. Our so-called stealing of this country from them was just a matter of survival. There were great numbers of people who needed new land, and the Indians were selfishly trying to keep it for themselves.

—John Wayne,
(political commentary and <u>not</u> from movie dialogue)

In 2016, looking back on those days, Bob Winter told me that he, Mickey, George Henningsen, and Joseph W. Carlini (both former New Jersey Casino Control Commission regulators and later chairmen of the Tribe's Gaming Commission) were focused almost exclusively on preventing organized crime infiltration of Foxwoods as the primary focus of a compact.

"Skip Heywood, who was the Tribal Chairman, wanted absolute assurance that there would be no infiltration by organized crime, and he wanted the compact to reflect that," Winter told me.

"In the early days of Tribal gaming there were constantly attempts in food services, hotel, vendors, everywhere; these unscrupulous people trying to get involved. And they may have got into some casinos; but not at Foxwoods, I am sure of that. The first compact built in guidelines almost as strict as New Jersey," he said.

"There are some great stories of how they tried to get in and things we found; but we were always one step ahead of them," he continued, explaining how that first compact made it possible for them to exert internal controls.

"Once after John Gotti had gone to prison, we got word from the FBI that Junior Gotti and some of his people were planning a big meeting at Foxwoods. So they came. We had recording devices, hidden cameras, video, everything. We knew everything they did," he remembered.

"Everybody knows that Las Vegas keeps a book of exclude persons that can't come into casinos. Well, we did the same thing; we had our list too. We kept those elements out of Foxwoods," he added.

Bob Winter's seemingly non-sequitur, if not obsessive, focus on keeping organized crime out of Indian country was not as fanatical as it might appear. Many Tribal leaders insisted on strict internal controls, background investigations, and financial history from anyone wanting to work for or do business with the Tribe. Native America had learned, the hard way, the necessity of such scrutiny. Thus, it was no coincidence that for the first Tribal compact and full-fledged casino, the Pequot leadership tapped top law enforcement officials deeply experienced in shutting down organized crime.

Visionary Tribal leaders like Skip Hayward, James Billie, and Max Osceola knew well that the Native history of relations with white people had been wrought with land-grabs, scams, financial schemes, and swindles against Indians. Long before sleazy white traders began selling alcohol to Indians, there were unscrupulous "business" dealings from Europeans settling in the "new world." For decades, the official policy of the United States Government included looting Indian country; Andrew Jackson's notorious "Trail of Tears" was spurred by the discovery of gold in north Georgia and white speculators' "need" of Creek and Cherokee land. Far beyond "buying" Manhattan for $24 worth of beads, the lure of billions of casino dollars has bred some creative, and sometimes absurd, schemes to steal from Native Americans.

No one was more aware of the schemes than those Tribal leaders at the birth of modern Indian Gaming. Infiltration began almost immediately, and so did Tribal vigilance against it.

"It was mostly management companies and financing deals," Bob Winter recalled thirty years later.

"In those days no traditional bank would finance these bingo casino deals for Tribes. Gambling was seen as a gray area of the law, before

IGRA; and the prohibition of a bank having a security interest on a reservation loan made it impossible at the time," he continued.

"So what you had were some of these really shady characters offering financial deals at exorbitant percentages of revenue; and there was no Federal legislation or Tribal Gaming Commissions at that time to protect the Tribal assets," he said.

As Winter remembered his early vigilance, I told him about a scam I had discovered at an Oklahoma casino 15 years after his trailblazing regulatory work for the Pequot Tribe. In reviewing contracts between the Tribe and its slot machine suppliers, I discovered a previously mentioned contract that paid the vendor 60% of the casino revenue in exchange for providing three doublewide trailers to the Tribe. To make matters worse, the contract contained an "evergreen" clause, meaning that the contract never expired, as long as the vendor changed at least one game title once every three years.

As if all this were not bad enough, it allowed that the vendor could cancel the contract at any time by giving the casino a 30-day written notice but the casino could never cancel the contract as long as the vendor met its obligation to change one game title. The one exception outlined in the contract was defined as "material breach." Specifically, the contract stated, "In the event of a material breach *by either party*, *either party* may notify the other party of said breach and *either party* may terminate this agreement immediately by notifying the other party either verbally or in writing of said breach by either party."

As I noted to Bob, clearly whoever had written this mumbo-jumbo was not a lawyer or at least not a competent one. I decided to challenge the company, and I had my secretary call the vendor's representatives to meet with the head of the Tribal Gaming Commission and me.

At the meeting I informed the vendor, "I want to report a material breach of the contract and we have to cancel the agreement immediately."

"Oh my God, what breach? There is no way" he asked assertively, and followed-up with an arrogance that had clearly been practiced to intimidate.

"Well, I am not going to pay you anymore," I smirked, suspecting that since the contract was not written by an attorney, the vendor would have no concept of the "constructive breach" that I was performing.

"You have 48 hours to get your machines out of my casino; after that time, I will have them removed from Indian trust land and placed on State Highway 9. Now get the fuck off Tribal land, you goddamn thieves. The days of stealing from this Tribe's members are over; there is a new sheriff in town and YOU are busted," I barked, trying to out-arrogant him.

Rather than back down, he threatened to "repossess" the doublewide trailers. Armed with the Bryan v. Itasca County decision and 20 years of Indian Gaming precedent since then, I finally won the arrogance war.

"If you step onto Tribal land and attempt such an illegal action, not only will you be met by Tribal Police and Bureau of Indian Affairs Police, but we will request assistance from the United States Marshall Service and will have you arrested for theft from a government reservation," I snorted.

I won the day and the Tribe saved tens of thousands if not hundreds of thousands of dollars. I had decades of case law and regulatory precedent behind me; but Bob Winter and those first-generation regulators were totally winging it with the first iteration of Federal regulations and very early Tribal controls. Also, in Bob's early days the threats were much more organized-crime-like than in later years, probably because Bob's colleagues were so successful in creating regulatory structures.

It is clear, nonetheless, that at least some degree of the "gangster infiltration" cited by government investigators was the product of vivid imaginations, anti-gaming paranoia, and anti-Indian attitudes in general. A 1990 never-publically released government memo revealed the depths of federal fanaticism about pre-IGRA Tribal bingo operations, while at the same time demonstrating typical disregard for Indian welfare.

A secret communique from Department of Interior Inspector General's Easter Regional Special-Agent-In-Charge, Daniel F. Lane, charged organized crime infiltration of Seminole Bingo in Hollywood Florida and at the same time recommended inactivity on the supposed mafia control.

Lane wrote, "A preliminary investigation of bingo operations revealed a relationship between the management personal, a known organized crime boss in southern Florida, and an organized crime family."

Addressed to the "Assistant Inspector General for Investigations Attn: Investigative Analyst, Easter Region," the copy of the memo leaked to me, 26 years after it was written, redacted the names of the crime boss and the crime family as well the names of an FBI Supervisory Special Agent in Miami and a Special Agent of the IRS in Fort Lauderdale. My own subsequent interviews, a discussion with Bob Winter, a reading of a major organized crime report, and an investigation by the Broward County Florida Sheriff's Department, provide a litany of organized crime allegations, innuendos, rumors, and (at best) sketchy contentions of shady business connections.

Invoking such pop-culturally chilling icons as Meyer Lansky, the Lucchese crime family, the 1957 Apalachin New York Mafia Commission meeting, and even President Lyndon Johnson's scandal-plagued aid Bobby Baker, the government alleges immense organized crime infiltration of the Seminole bingo operations.

Yet, after pages of bad-movie-like allegations of mobsters running havoc over the Tribal bingo halls, the memo concludes, "a complete investigation of the bingo operation would require at least two agents involved in a full time effort, the utilization of an undercover agent or operative, and Title III surveillance capabilities. Due to the lack of resources, I recommend that the case be closed administratively." And it was.

With the benefit of hindsight, a 21st century reader has to wonder if it really would have been too great of a resource drain to add two agents in order capture so many mafia luminaries in a South Florida dragnet. In that retrospection, one has to wonder if this was more of "round up the usual suspects" than actual evidence of a problem.

Chief James Billie said, basically, the same thing when news of the "investigation" was leaked to a local newspaper and the reporter called him to comment. The Chief brushed off the investigations as hearsay with no substantiated evidence of any kind. What the Chief did not bother to tell reporters was that, according to Lane, the investigation was triggered by a request from the Tribal government. According to

Lane, the Seminole Tribe had contacted his office on October 17, 1987 to look into the possibility of their first management company skimming profits at the Hollywood Florida bingo hall. Still, he recommended administratively closing the case.

All of that does not necessarily indicate that there was no actual organized crime interest in the Tribal operation; but it does raise questions about the quality of investigations and the motivation behind some of the allegations. At the very least, it seems clear that the pre-IGRA Tribal bingo hall had become a lightning rod for all manner of anti-Indian and anti-gambling interests.

For example, one "investigation" reported by the Florida Sun Sentinel newspaper questioned the legitimacy of Max Osceola's salary, expense account, and even personal IRS bill, all without bothering to compare him to his counterparts in similar-sized publically traded gaming companies. The insinuation was that there was something untoward going on; but closer inspection found him to be vastly undercompensated by comparison.

Likewise, one government "Organized Crime Commission" investigative report claimed that the Tribe's Hollywood Florida management company was making regular tribute payments to the LaRocca family in Pittsburgh. That investigation reported that mobsters were skimming $400 to $500 a month from the bingo hall. Again, it seems, at best, implausible that from a $20-million-a-year enterprise, these big-time gangsters would be content with a monthly tribute that was less than they spent for a box of cigars.

Despite such dubiously generated allegations, Lieutenant David Green of the Broward County (Florida) Sheriff's Department told a 1988 Senate committee that Meyer Lansky with the New York Lucchese and the Pennsylvania Bufalino crime families had funded the Seminole's bingo hall. Years later, Bob Winter echoed, "the Lucchese crime family was involved and so were a lot of other notorious crime figures."

At least Winter's assertion came from a substantial investigative source; an April 1992 report on *Racketeering and Organized Crime in the Bingo Industry*, written by the Pennsylvania Crime Commission.

"Tribes and regulations were not nearly as sophisticated in those early days as they are now. It was nothing like today. There were no rules," laments Buddy Levy, whose company competed with the target of that investigation. Levy's company ran the Tampa property while the targeted company ran Hollywood Florida's Seminole Bingo, the original *Seminole Tribe v. Butterworth* birthplace of Tribal casinos.

Levy acknowledges that there were investigations at the time and many operators and Tribes were unaware of what was going on. "It turned out that some real gangsters were involved in some things," he recalled.

As true as the Levy-Clare model was the template for legitimate financing and gaming management, a company called "Seminole Management Associates Ltd." was, according to the investigators, the template for organized crime infiltration. Formed in May of 1979, the company's Florida State filing documents listed five general partners: Eugene Weisman, the J.B. Cooper Trust, Simon Investment Corp., and Lawrence Schine.

According to the Pennsylvania investigation, Larry Schine and George Simon were executives of a small Miami-based hotel chain. The J.B. Cooper Trust, the report claims, was operated by reputed Miami arms dealer Jack Cooper. Cooper, remembered for being implicated in the Bobby Baker bribery scandal during the Johnson presidency, was long thought to be a close associate of Meyer Lansky. A May 1974 report from the U.S. Department of Justice's Organized Crime and Racketeering Section identified Cooper as the "courier of Las Vegas skim money for Lansky in early 60's" and a part of the "Lansky entourage."

Pennsylvania was involved in the investigation because of Weisman's participation. The report positions Eugene Weisman as a strawman for the LaRocca family, alleging that he funneled Seminole bingo money to family boss Sonny Ciancutti and capo Kelly Mannarino.

Gabriel "Kelly" Mannarino was a Pittsburgh-based LaRocca captain who had represented the family at the historic 1957 Apalachin New York Mafia Commission meeting. Closely associated with Florida mob boss Santo Trafficante, Mannarino was in charge of the LaRocca casino interests in Cuba as well as collections from gambling halls throughout Pennsylvania. The report identified one of the bingo halls under Mannarino's LaRocca rule as an East Pittsburgh hall owned by Weisman.

Ciancutti, the reputed boss of the Pittsburgh family, began his career as a craps dealer for one Mannarino's illegal casinos. The FBI says that Ciancutti served as "consigliere" to the Pittsburgh family from 2002 until 2006 and then became Underboss to Godfather John Bazzano; following Bazzano's death in 2008, Ciancutti allegedly became the boss of the Pittsburgh family.

According to the report, the Tribe had hoped to finance the building of the casino from the success of the Tribe's drive-through cigarette business. However, the BIA and banks refused funding for a bingo hall, again citing a bank's inability to foreclose on sovereign land. The Pennsylvania report claims that Weisman took a $1.2 million investment from Lansky to start Seminole Management Associates to finance and construct the Butler building-style bingo hall building. The loan, according to the report, came from Lanksy, the Lucchese Family from New York, the Bufalino crime family in Scranton Wilkes-Barre Pennsylvania, and the LaRocca family in Pittsburgh.

The problem with this Mario-Puzo-worthy movie-script drama is that outside of the associations and friendships, it conflicts with the actual facts of how the bingo hall came into existence. The paper trail created at the time, by Max Osceola and the Bureau of Indian Affairs, shows a radically different version of the founding of the bingo hall. Rather than vulture-like Lansky-driven mobsters circling naïve Tribes and randomly picking the Seminole, reality shows a successful cigarette-business Tribe looking for ways to expand their revenue by adding a bingo hall to their portfolio.

This latter scenario is further supported in Buddy Levy's discussion of why the Seminole did not follow the Pequot model of petitioning the State for a compact. Tribes in Minnesota and Wisconsin immediately followed the Pequot model and Levy urged the Seminole to do the same.

"In those early days, the States thought they had to sign a compact no matter what," Levy recalled.

"I wanted the (Seminole) Tribe to immediately submit a compact to Florida; but the Tribe's lobbyists told them that the state would retaliate against the Tribe by taking away the Seminole's agreement with the State that allowed the tax-free sale of cigarettes on sovereign land. That represented about $13 million a year in revenue and the lobbyists convinced the (Tribal) Council that a compacted casino would never make that much. For $13 million, they walked away from hundreds of millions, likely billions by now," he explained.

"It turned out that those lobbyists were playing both sides against the middle. They represented the Tribe, but they also represented interests that did not want to see full-blown Las Vegas style casinos in Florida; they represented horse tracks and out-of-state gambling companies," he lamented, adding, with a sigh, "billions of dollars for Tribal programs."

That reluctance by the Tribe seems to support the contention that the bingo operation was more of a supplemental economic development program, as Max Osceola insisted, than some elaborate La Cosa Nostra conspiracy for Meyer Lansky's fortunes.

Nevertheless, the Pennsylvania and Federal investigations did correctly identify some associations between the principals of Seminole Management and a number of characters well known for organized crime. Those associations were much more loose than, for example, the associations between President Kennedy's father bootlegging during prohibition with some of the founders of the New York "five families" of the mafia or even the founders of today's large publically held casino and slot machine companies.

As Levy accurately noted, in those pre-IGRA days there were no gaming commissions, prohibitions of friendships or "guilt by association" guidelines, limits on revenue-share percentages, nor restrictions on sources of capital. Those were regulatory restrictions later imposed by IGRA, 25 C.F.R., and Tribal Gaming Authorities. Corollary to that, none of the associations cited in the investigations were illegal or particularly unusual. Interestingly enough, none of the investigative reports cited any actual illegal activity around the Seminole project. While conjectures of intent are impossible, it does seem clear that the motivation of the loan investment seemed to be to share in the substantial projected revenue from the gambling operation.

Although IGRA arbitrarily limited revenue share management agreements to 30%, in the pre-IGRA days there were no limits and the Seminole Management Associates deal was for 45% of the net profit. With a $20 million annual revenue, that was a tidy $9 million a year for Weisman's company, for a 20-year contract that represented $180 million against a $1.2 million investment. Nowhere else was that kind of return possible for bankers, mobsters, or anyone else. In light of that kind of legitimate return on investment, it seems unlikely that "organized crime," or anyone else on the investment side, would have much of an appetite for standard mafia skims or other such crimes.

Nonetheless, once IGRA passed and its restrictions on sovereign decision-making kicked in, the government determined that the bingo hall was in violation of the management contract regulations of the National Indian Gaming Commission (NIGC). Three years earlier through a series of complex and often bureaucratic maneuvers, the Tribe bought out the Seminole Management Associates contract (for $60 million) after investors in the company failed IGRA-mandated background checks. Weisman's brother "Skip" created a company, JPW Consultants, to sign a replacement management agreement, and in response, the NIGC levied the largest fine in its history, $3.4 million, against JPW for failure to get NIGC approval of the new deal.

Despite all the chest-pounding and accusation-throwing government assaults on the Tribe's bingo operations, ultimately the only actual violation was a procedural issue with the management company and absolutely nothing against the Tribe. In fact, in the three-decade history of IGRA and the much older history of Indian Gaming, there has never been a proven mafia infiltration or skim of an Indian casino.

Of much greater concern, and law enforcement focus, *should* be the scores and scores of "unorganized" crimes that plague casinos everywhere, whether they are Indian or commercial. Similar to that Oklahoma upside-down contract and doublewide trailer scam that I had halted, an uncountable number of low-level swindles infect (or attempt to infect) casinos every year. Most are textbook rip-offs with an occasional new twist; or at least a new perpetrator of the age-old scams and rip-offs of Indians.

These small-scale, less-headline-grabbing schemes steal more every year than any imagined infiltration by a mythical Don Corleone. Typically, a quick security or operational audit can determine which of the age-old schemes is being used to rip off the casino and Tribal assets. It is very rare to find these small-time bandits versed in more complex schemes or even in more than one swindle at a time, but it occasionally happens.

A few years ago I found a true microcosm of almost every imaginable casino rip-off; living testimony to the necessity of the Bob-Winter-style regulatory controls. Far beyond merely one Tribe's uniquely sloppy controls, what I found was insight into an industry-wide problem that begged for attention, an active "graduate school" of how to steal from a Tribal casino.

My immersion began when an Oklahoma Tribal Treasurer called me to help determine why his Tribe's casino was not making money. Despite being one of the state's most high-profile casinos with huge crowds every night, the casino was actually *losing* money. Every month, just to meet payroll, the casino borrowed about $16,000 from the Tribal treasury. The Tribal Executive Council wanted me to conduct an operational audit of the should-be-successful casino and determine why there was a loss and why outside audits had revealed only "flat" revenue for the past three years.

With promotions that included some of the biggest names in country music performing at the casino, the former head coach of the University of Oklahoma appearing to sign autographs, and over-top giveaways of luxury cars and motorcycles, the casino was drawing weekday crowds of 1,000 to 1,500 players and weekend crowds of 6,000 to 8,000 gamblers. The casino boasted about 900 slot machines, a 1,000+ seat concert venue, a 24-hour restaurant, a gift shop, a full service bar, and one of only two sports racing books in the entire state. At least on paper, there was no theoretical reason the casino should not have been profitable; and certainly no excuse for having to borrow money from an already impoverished Tribe.

Despite a personal distaste for the Midwest, in general, (yes, I DO call them "fly-over states"), and my reluctance to leave a highly successful run with Donald Trump, I accepted the invitation from the Treasurer to venture into the Class-II-only State of Oklahoma. In advance of my arrival, I asked that a paper trail of documents be assembled for me to review and for the treasurer to assign someone to accompany me on a detailed physical inspection of the property.

It was not until I arrived in Oklahoma that the treasurer told me that in addition to the losses, the Tribe had been fined (presumably by the National Indian Gaming Commission) for management's illegal operation of blackjack tables in the state which prohibited them. The Tribe had been given three years to pay off the multimillion dollar fine.

One of those paper trails provided by the Tribe was a huge American Express bill. The treasurer told me that the casino's General Manager had opened an American Express account in the casinos' name without the Tribal Council's knowledge or consent and had issued cards to several employees. I later learned that the former Governor of the Tribe, who had died in office, authorized the accounts. His administrative assistant told me, however, that he was bedridden and not aware of what he was signing at the time the manager visited him in a hospital with the forms to sign.

Additionally, several marketing department employees had confessed that they had purchased personal clothing and household furnishings from department stores, charging the items to casino accounts authorized by the Director of Marketing (who was married to the General Manager). So there was a paper trail there, as well.

The NIGC fine, these bills, questionable management practices in general, and a pretty fat staff (the marketing department alone had almost 20 "managers") all combined to paint a clear picture of the financial status of the business. Given that picture, I added to my inquiry list a report of the actual operating costs as well as the daily cash flow, including cash-in and payouts to winners.

I also wanted to review, in detail, the "flat" casino audits for the past three years. IGRA and 25. C.F.R. require that Indian casinos annually submit to an independent outside audit. This Tribe had contracted with one of the most respected accounting firms in the industry; however, the audits were a woeful disappointment. The last pages, for each year, detailed the casino management's refusal to release financial data and refusal to give any information access to auditors. The treasurer was baffled and the audits were worthless; they had no data. *Something* was definitely up.

After reviewing the limited amount of paper evidence, I met David Cook, a bulldog retired cop; in fact, he was the most decorated living police officer in the history of Oklahoma. After leaving the Oklahoma City Police Department on a medical early retirement (his lungs had been scorched during the raid of a methamphetamine lab), he had been hired by the Tribe to head their Gaming Commission. He was also assigned to be my tour guide, leading me around the casino, introducing me to staff, and briefing me on what he had discovered in his own investigations.

Before my arrival, Cook fired the General Manager; and the GM had already fired his own wife when he was "shocked to discover that she misused the American Express account." (*Shades of Rick Blane paying Louie's gambling winnings just as Louie was ordering Café Americain closed!*)

My first stop was the GM's former office, which still had a cloud of stale cigarette smoke hovering in the air. The desk was coated with a thick, yellow, sticky film of nicotine and when I rested the side of my hand on it, my palm became coated with a yellow stain. I instinctively looked around the room for a smoke detector, and not only found none but also noted there were no security cameras there either, a little odd.

I had already observed that the separate administration building was a two-story wooden-frame structure with no sprinkler system nor smoke detectors, and most of the employees in that building smoked at their desks. Several of the offices had burning cigarettes in ashtrays but no one in the office. Walking through the casino to the GM's office with David Cook, I noticed there was no fire suppression or sprinkler system over most of the area. And so my inspection began.

Just outside the rear entrance to the casino, I saw a parked, long refrigeration trailer (apparently, from an 18-wheel tractor-trailer rig). Electric wires ran from the casino to power the refrigeration unit on the truck. There was a small padlock on the doors to the trailer. Cook told me that he had put the padlock on the trailer after learning that it had at one time been totally filled with frozen restaurant-quality steaks and no lock on the doors. When he opened those doors for me, there was only one pallet of the meat left; in less than two months the small casino and its tiny coffee shop had gone through an entire truck load of steaks. OR...with the door not having a lock and no surveillance camera in the back of the casino, someone possibly had been stealing the meat. That was one of the oldest rackets in stealing from a restaurant. I think Nicholas Pileggi detailed that scam in *Wise Guys* as did Demaris Ovid in *The Last Mafioso; Jimmy the Weasel Fratianno*. This was the first time I had actually seen it in action. I just shook my head.

As I walked along the outside of the casino, I noticed electrical wires and CAT-5 network cable looped along the side of the building without conduit or even ties. Subsequent examination revealed that these were the cables that carried the game outcomes (from the virtual bingo draw) from the server rooms to the slot machines. I asked Cook, "What is to keep someone from splicing into one of those lines and changing the outcome of the game?"

"You mean like that?" he responded as he pointed to a ball of black plastic electrical tape wrapped around an obvious splice point. "Oh you haven't seen anything yet," Cook told me as he read the pained expression on my face.

I scanned the parking lot and the back acreage of the property, looking for backup generators (in the event of loss of power). Running 900 server-based slot machines could be a big problem if customers had money in play during a power outage; unless there was a generator in place to pick up where a local UPS would fail. Most casino *Minimum Internal Control Standards* required backup generators. Here there was no such requirement and no generators.

As we walked toward the door to go back inside, I got a hefty whiff of what smelled like a freshly fertilized field. I looked at Cook who laughed and led me to an open cesspool. "Please don't tell me that is the raw sewerage from the casino," I almost pleaded.

"Totally legal here; you are on a sovereign nation," he reminded me, adding "it is only bad when the wind changes direction."

"Shit," I said. "Exactly," David laughed.

As soon as we stepped back inside the casino, David pointed me toward two closets near the back door. Each had a series of barn-hinge hasps with padlocks through them. I thought of one of my New York City apartments as I counted eight different locks on each door. Cook, who had a ring of keys that looked like something the high school janitor used to carry around, did not have the keys to these secure closets. He pointed to the hinges on the doors and scratch marks indicating that the pins in the hinges had been repeatedly removed so that the door could be opened without unlocking.

The NIGC, trying to effectively protect Tribal assets, required that the virtual ping-pong-ball bingo servers be locked away from the general public and required: ...*physical security measures restricting access to agents, including vendors, must exist over the servers, including computer terminals, storage media, software and data files to prevent unauthorized access and loss of integrity of data and processing.* These two closets were the "secure sever rooms" for the casino.

"Do I EVEN want to see this," I asked Cook, rhetorically.

He called for the "IT Department" to allow us access. I can't think of the words to describe what I saw in these closets. For my older readers, you will remember the sound of the contents of Lum and Abner's closet falling out when the door opened. For younger readers, imagine a closet packed with wires, old computers (working and not working), oily rags, scraps of paper, half-empty soft drink cans, molded coffee floating in months-old cups, broken furniture parts, and even a mousetrap with peanut butter bait. Imagine all of that balanced so that if the door opened too quickly, everything would lose balance and fall out the door. Add to that lovely visual, a spider-web of network cables, unlabeled or otherwise identified, each coming from a network hub underneath one of the banks of slot machines. Approximately 75 cables were strung to one (or both) of the closets, all without conduit or labels. The cables were draped, pulled, looped, and strung seemingly haphazardly and intertwined through each other without organization. I cringed and continued my tour.

As I walked across the gaming floor toward a section of the casino called the "Nickel Corral," I tripped on a weak section of the floor (and wondered about slip-and-fall accidents).

"Oh that is where the forklift fell through the floor when it was lifting the sculpture to the top of those slot machines," a housekeeping employee told me, adding "people fall there all the time. We just never got it fixed." The treasurer had already told me that the casino had spent $75,000 to buy a solid bronze sculpture from an Oklahoma Seminole Nation leader (who was also a state senator) as a sort of political tribute.

The " nickel corral," I discovered, was not actually part of the casino structure; rather, it was made of four doublewide mobile home trailers stitched together and attached to a side doorway from the main casino. (This was a common casino construction technique for Oklahoma Indian casinos in those days.) In this section, the lights had been taken out and replaced with one "black light" tube in every other fixture. The room was so dark that I could see the people at slot machines only because of the glow of the slot machine video screens and not from room lighting. The room was dangerously dark and the construction of the trailers did not seem solid enough to support the weight of the slot machines; the floor buckled as I walked across it (and I only weighed 160 pounds at the time).

I scanned the room for security cameras, hoping that surveillance officers had a good view of the room and the machines. There were smoked bubbles for the cameras, but I seriously doubted that anyone could see an image through cameras (if there even were any) because of the darkness.

I looked at the front of the slot machines and noticed that many of the machines did not have locks on the compartments that housed the cash. This meant that an unscrupulous customer or dishonest employee could open the front of the slot machine, and get to the cash drop box.

As I opened the glass door on one machine, I discovered there was no lock on the cash box either. This meant that not only could anyone reach the cash box, but they could get to the cash as well. I glanced up to the camera covers and again realized that even during a drop, there would be no way to observe cash taken from the machines. I wondered how much had been out-and-out stolen. I also noted that the mere action of opening that glass door should have triggered surveillance alarms, apparently it did not.

Since I was already inside the machine, without a key, I checked the audit meters...or rather I tried to check the meters. There were none. Hence, there was no physical record (hard meters) of how much cash went into the machine or was paid out; it was as if these machines had been designed to be stolen from. This would have been totally illegal in Nevada and in most Indian casinos nationwide.

I closed the slot machine door, shook my head again, and turned to David to continue my tour. As I slammed the machine shut, I commented, "These are some seriously fucked-up slot machines." A nearby slot technician ran up to me and warned, "You are not allowed to call these slot machines, you have to call them video gaming devices."

"Horseshit. They are Class II slot machines," I said. The tech replied, "we were told to never call them that, it is a secret. We have to call them video machines."

"A secret? You were told that by an asshole. What you call the machines does not change what they are or what they are not. They ARE slot machines; just Class II type slot machines." I argued as I walked to the front of the room.

That consumer deception technically continues today; as recently as May of 2016, I was a speaker at a conference on Class II games and two manufacturers' representatives "corrected" my calling them slot machines, objecting that if I called them slot machines they might be subject to slot machine scrutiny. It is a ruse that I have never accepted, but was even more common in those days.

I continued my tour. At the front of those trailer rooms, there was a construction area that looked like it had at one time been the bathrooms for the mobile homes. Workers had installed a bullet-resistant Plexiglas window and were busying themselves measuring for sheet rock walls. Inside the construction area I could see the Cage and Cashier Manager directing the work crew. As I opened the hollow door to step into the room with Cook, the manager asked me what I thought of the new location of their "satellite" cage. Hiding my shock, all I could immediately respond was, "ah...No."

The Federal Register has published (in 25 C.F.R. Chapter 500) a detailed set of Minimum Internal Control Standards (MICS) for protecting Tribal assets at a casino; these are minimum standards that I keep referencing here, and they are very detailed. It was those standards that had made me cringe at the "server room" closets and the dangling wiring outside the building. Most of the issues I cited on my tour were minor violations of those MICS.

This violation, however, was totally absurd. A casino cashiers' cage is the "bank" inside the casino; however, in an average day a cage handles a lot more money than a typical branch bank. There are very specific guidelines (as well as common sense) about how such an area is to be secured. Drop ceiling panels, hollow doors, paper-thin trailer walls, and pressed-wood floors above cinder blocks do not really make for the most secure of banks. Frankly, I thought they were joking when they told me that this area was going to be a bank/cage.

"How exactly are you going to protect the Tribe's cash in this configuration?" I rhetorically asked no one.

Years later, when I developed a casino for the Ottawa Tribe of Oklahoma (the diametrical opposite of THIS Tribe in terms of functionality, integrity, and harmony), I personally wrote a set of Tribal Internal Controls (TICS) that was adopted by their gaming commission, approved by the NIGC, is still in use today, and has been copied by me many times over the years for less-regulated casinos. Those controls, very specifically, define protection of the cage and the Tribe's cash.

I continued my tour through the casino, stopping long enough to admire an indoor rock waterfall with ivy growing through it. "I wouldn't get too close to that," a maintenance man warned me, "just a couple of months ago we found a momma rattler had hatched six baby rattlesnakes there." I turned to Cook, who just shrugged his shoulders as he continued my tour.

Our next stop was through a doorway that led to a bar and a racing book; a classic OTB (off track betting) parlor with wide screen televisions, a remote access "Amtote" race-betting machine, and lots of trophy cups, jockey colors, and track decoration (as well as a full service bar). It was, truly, a beautifully designed room. I immediately spotted a guy handicapping races for a number of players and then collecting a percentage of their winnings as a toke.

"Who is the tic-tac artist?" I asked Cook. "The what?" he responded. "The dude working the room for a cut of the winnings," I said pointing to the guy.

"Oh, that is the manager of our OTB," David explained. "Get-the-fuck-outta-here," I heard myself say in Trump-esque slang. Great, the manager of the OTB is illegally handicapping for players. Never mind the ethical violations of that; never mind the MICS violations of licensed employees participating in the outcome of a bet; it is just a sleazy-looking practice. I shook my head and made another mental note.

I watched two of the barmaids return "spillage" (that had not spilled at all) and pocket the price of the drink themselves without hitting the cash register. Even the bar was ripe with criminal pilferage. Behind the bar and in a side room I examined the rack and gun system and observed the inventory setup. I would bet dollars-to-donut-holes that the inventory was being short-reported. (I later learned that not only was that true, but the alcohol distributor was giving cash kickbacks to at least two of the bar shift managers for their orders.) *And why in the hell had the surveillance department not caught THAT?*

As we continued the tour, we walked through the main casino through another set of glass doors and into the bingo hall. Behind me was a balcony overlooking the room. As I climbed the stairway toward the balcony I could feel each step give a little and I listened to the creak each time I put weight on a step. The balcony itself bowed and bent as I walked across the floor, so much so that I really didn't want to be up there. This balcony had been built, Cook said, for dozens of VIPS and special guests to sit during concerts that were periodically held in the bingo hall/showroom. I later learned that this balcony was built on one-inch by two-inch support beams (rather than two-by-fours) holding sheets of plywood, with no additional support. The carpenter, who had built this substandard accident-waiting-to-happen, was overheard in a local bar laughing about that and other objects of his work, saying "I stole so much money from those Indians and delivered them shit. I hope that doesn't change with the new guy there." He was in for an unpleasant surprise.

At the far end of the bingo hall was a stage, about 12 to 15 feet above the floor. The bingo hall indeed was designed to double as an auditorium for concerts but rather than looking down at the stage, customers had to crane their necks to look up to see the performers. Those sitting closest to the stage could see nothing at all, and those in the flimsy balcony at the back of the room had the best view.

As we walked around the stage we discovered three doors, two in the front of the stage and one behind the stage. David had keys to the two front doors and behind each we found large rooms filled with folding metal chairs, most likely used to convert the room into a concert hall. But David did not have a key to the back door and neither did casino security or the Tribal police. With a sledgehammer, we broke the lock on that door and discovered a plush, carpeted, sound-proof room with couches, beds, refrigerator (filled with beer), televisions, paintings on the walls, and a telephone that did not go through the casino switchboard. The room looked like a giant hotel suite, but contained the stale smell of burned marijuana, warm beer, and assorted musk.

Subsequent investigation of the phone revealed that a "secret" phone line had been installed with a separate bill sent directly to the casino (rather than to Tribal headquarters). A review of the past year's bill showed more than $100,000 in long distance charges to locations all over the world. We later learned that the room itself had been furnished for some female members of the marketing staff to "entertain" performers, roadies, and other "special guests" who might enjoy the carnal pleasures of the marketing girls. This casino had it all!

Behind the stage was another door…for which, like the secret room, no one could find a key. The solid wooden door had a deadbolt lock and the closest locksmith was two days from getting to us. I made the executive decision to have the door kicked in. Behind that door was the entrance to an entirely different world from the rustic casino. A hallway led to a private entrance hidden off the north side of the building; apparently a "secret" entrance for entertainers arriving on tour buses or by limo. (The casino's limo, incidentally, had disappeared and there was no record of it ever existing.)

Off the hallway were two luxurious "dressing rooms," one obviously for the "star" and one for the "band." Both were thickly carpeted and had large private bathrooms and showers. They were well-lit, had modern walls, and expensive ceramic tile leading to the carpeted rooms. Thinking about returning to the nicotine-poisoned General Manager's office, I turned to Cook and one of the maintenance men and said, "welcome to my new office." I quickly gave instructions for cutting a doorway between the two rooms, putting a buzzer-controlled see-through glass security door where we had crashed through, dividing one room into a receptionist room and large boardroom, and turning the other room into an executive office. Ok, now at least I would not have to be detoxed every time I walked into my office.

As I walked back through the bingo hall/showroom, I was almost overcome with a thick smoke cloud that had covered the room in the short time since I had walked through. The smoke was billowing through a large vent in the back side of the hall, spewing like an open fire and filling the room with a noxious greasy smell. Subsequent exploration revealed that the "hood" over the deep fryer and grill in the kitchen did not work and the smoke had been rerouted into this bingo hall. A close look at the wall, where the vent was located, revealed a fire hazard of caked grease dripping...or oozing...from the vent. Yuck.

Next stop on my tour was the "admin" building; the casino offices in an out building. There was no covered walkway between the casino and that building; I guessed that in rain or snow employees just covered their heads and ran from the offices to the casino. I had already seen many people smoking in the two-story wooden frame building (with no fire suppression nor smoke detectors), but it was not until I toured the building office-by-office that I realized how flimsy and "trailer-like" the construction was. The stairway to the second floor shook and creaked like the stairway to the balcony in the showroom; and the second story itself caved and dipped as I walked across it. I could see bows in the floor where file cabinets or desks weighted it.

Removed from the casino building, it was obvious that the occupants of this building lived by their own rules and in their own little world. That rogue marketing department was housed in and ruled from this building, away from any curious Tribal eyes that might visit the casino.

I immediately spotted a court-required ankle bracelet on one of the marketing employees. As Cook noticed that I was staring at it, he told me that the girl was a convicted felon (drugs and assault) who had served "hard prison time" and was now on house arrest. Though she could not "technically" be licensed to work in a casino, she was a relative of a high-ranking Tribal official. I glanced at a charming tattoo across her right forearm that read, "Fuck You Bitch," and I continued my tour.

The rest of the administration building was a continuation of faulty construction, bad plumbing, coughing-heavy smoke, and nepotism in key positions.

The final stop on my property tour was another out-building; a long Quonset-hut looking storage building. At first glance, it looked like a storage building for lawn mowers, ground equipment, and various parts and supplies. However, a more detailed examination revealed a universe of marketing supplies, two $20,000 go-carts, and a wealth of high-value "prizes" for players.

Most notable among the discarded displays and promotional items were banners and stands for several antique Harley Davidson motorcycles. According to the treasurer, in later investigation, the former GM had purchased the bikes at an auction from the Venetian in Vegas following the closing Guggenheim's *The Art of the Motorcycle* collection of motorcycles dating from a steam-powered cycle of 1868 at the Venetian. The treasurer told me that the motorcycles had been purchased to be awarded in contest drawings for players but had been "won" by the carpenter (who did the questionable work) and the GM himself. Whether his allegations were true or false will probably never be known since there was no paper trail for the winners (which by the way is another MICS violation itself).

With my property tour over, I set about reviewing contracts and relationships with slot machine vendors who were providing machines for the casino; a task I was already dreading because I had recognized the machines during my tour as being ones that were generally spurned by sophisticated casinos. The Tribe had a hard-and-fast rule against ever purchasing slot machines; they wanted revenue-share machine leases only. The treasurer's thinking was that the speed of technology would make purchased machines obsolete by the time they paid for themselves. An "expensive" new machine sold for about $13,000 at the time; an Oklahoma revenue share (at that time) was about 35% of win-per-unit. Hence, if a machine was averaging a win of $100 per day, then the vendor would get a rev share of $35 per day or $12,775 per year. Ellis felt that machine technology changed more frequently than that time frame. Unfortunately, most rev-share contracts were for a minimum of 3 years so that $13,000 slot machine actually cost the Tribe $38,000. Further complicating the situation, the machines at this casino were not $13,000 machines; they were (at most) $7,000 machines and would have paid for themselves in seven months. Nonetheless, the Tribe was firm on the rule and the property was filled with lease-only machines. I, thus, set about the task of reviewing those revenue-share leases.

As I have discussed, in Indian Gaming a typical casino rev-share deal was what we called an 80/20 split; of the "win," the casino would keep 80% and the vendor would be paid 20%. Typically, there were only two exceptions to that standard: (1) a slightly higher vendor share (up to a total of 27% at times) was paid for "premium" game titles (such as themed games for which manufacturers had to pay royalties for the theme license) and (2) an additional share (again totaling no more than 27%) for certain vendor-paid promotions or advertising.

Unfortunately, none of the "deals" in this casino's contracts were "typical." The previously discussed "upside down" contract was just one example of unorthodox, cheating, and illegal contracts under which the Tribe suffered. The next contract I reviewed revealed that the revenue share was a three-way split rather than a two-way. While I did not know of anything illegal or in violation of MICS about such an arrangement, it still waved a red flag at me warning that something was unusual. The language bothered me so much that I invited the vendor in to meet with me and discuss the contract.

This vendor's sale representative seemed sincere, honest, and very open about the contract. He explained, "Mr. Green, I have never seen anything like this either; let me tell you what happened. We came to see the officials here at this casino to pitch our games and they seemed to love them. In fact, the slot manager told me she wanted them on the floor immediately. I thought we had a deal and I told her that I would be back the next day with a contract. When I came back, I was told that unfortunately there was no floor space available for my machines because another vendor—the other name in your contract there—had signed an agreement for all of the remaining floor space. They went on to tell me that the other vendor had not used all of his allocated space and that perhaps he would give some of it up to me if I would call him directly. I called him and he agreed to sell me his floor space for 10% of the revenue of the machines. I had never heard of such a thing so I told the casino that if I was going to do such a thing I wanted it in the contract. That is why your rev share is with two companies, my percentage and the payoff to this other guy," he explained in obviously frustrated dismay.

"I later found out that of his 10% he only kept 5% and the other 5% was paid as marketing fees in personal checks to the casino's marketing director, who I think was married to the general manager here," he added.

I am able to so vividly report this conversation, years later, because this vendor became a close friend and eventually a business partner with me in several ventures. He reminds me of the details constantly and has told the story over and over to industry operatives. Also, the Tribal treasurer later confirmed that part of the story after he obtained copies of canceled checks as well as a contract between that third-party vendor and the GM's wife. The "other guy" who orchestrated this illegal scam, as of this writing, is a multimillionaire financier of Indian casinos with several currently active "exclusive floor space" deals under his belt. In bidding for various development deals in recent years, my main competitor has been that company... which never misses the opportunity to give their version of how I sabotaged Tribal funding nationwide by thwarting that and other contracts.

The next contract I reviewed had a clause that excused that vendor from providing paper for their machines' payout tickets. Again, I called for a sit-down with the vendor. He explained to me that he had offered to provide the paper, of course, but was told "by the casino" that his paper would not be accepted and that he should exclude it from the contract. When I asked him where the casino got paper for his machines, he cited a printing company in Nashville Tennessee.

A call to that company revealed that their contract was with a third-party company, which they revealed to have the same name and address as a company co-owned by the GM's wife and that other vendor who had "sold" floor space at the casino.

Another vendor, when I questioned his contract, warned me that if I questioned their percentage, the way he heard that I had done of other vendors, they would close the casino by repossessing the building. This was similar to the idle threat from the 60% contract vendor I had discussed with Bob Winter. It turned out that their company also had purchased doublewide trailers that became part of the casino structure. Apparently, they had been promised that their machines and only their machines would fill those trailers forever at whatever contractual arrangement they dictated. Equally apparently, these geniuses had used the same kind legal scholars that the other company had used, again overlooking Bryan v. Itasca.

Back in the bingo hall operation, I discovered extra charges on the bingo paper and supplies contracts, through a third-party vendor (rather than directly with one of the bingo vendors). The mark-ups would have been laughable if it had not been costing the casino so much money every week.

Another casino contract, this one with a bus company, provided that the casino pay the company $600 per trip to drive the 37 miles from Oklahoma City three times a week. Additionally, the casino paid the bus operators a bounty of $10 per person delivered to the casino. The casino also reimbursed the bus company for fuel (from presented diesel receipts) and provided each bus rider with $20 in free bingo play. Finally, the casino was required to pay for advertising the bus trips in the Oklahoma City newspaper (though no one I talked with had ever seen one of the alleged ads). I later learned that the "players" were picked up from homeless shelters in Oklahoma City and were required to split their winnings with the bus driver 50/50. The Tribal governor (Chief) told me that he witnessed a bus driver chase an elderly homeless woman through the parking lot and tackle her to the ground to collect his half of the $50 she had won one night.

Still another vendor's contract had a revenue share of 37.5% going to the vendor. The fine print explained that the actual revenue share was "only" 32.5% and the additional 5% was paid into a marketing fund, which was spent at the vendor's discretion and not the casino's. A phone call turned into one of the most paternalistic (if not racist) explanations I had heard in a long time: "you know, Mr. Green, a lot of these Tribes really aren't smart enough to know how to use marketing money, so we set this aside to make sure something gets done right."

Beyond the paternalistic nonsense, I was outraged that a slot machine company thought they were going to tell ME how to market a casino. Maybe they had not heard of Donald Trump and our marketing.

Throughout my reviews, not a single contract had the standard 80% to 20% revenue share. Moreover, not one of them had a rev share of less than 30% going to the vendor. (I later learned that no one in Oklahoma had "normal" rev shares.) None of the vendors were what I would have called "top-tier" slot machine companies (no IGT, Bally,

Aristocrat, WMS, and so on), and though IGT had not yet entered the Class II market there were plenty of legitimate vendors in the space.

Unfortunately, this casino seemed to have a lot more "questionable" vendors than legitimate ones. Even the top names in Class II (VGT, Rocket, etc.) were missing from the floor of this casino; presumably not willing to pay the kickback/extortion fees to the third-party company. The floor was plagued with machines from companies that existed only for Oklahoma and in two cases, companies created only for this one casino and on the surface at least quasi-criminal operations and at worst probably Racketeer Influenced and Corrupt Organizations.

I turned my orientation focus from the facility and the contracts to the staff, to human resources. Like the melodrama of corruption, I had seen in the building and in the contracts, I found the staffing to be (at best) below the acceptable Minimum Internal Control Standards, despite the fact that David Cook had already fired more than 100 employees. Nepotism was rampant; but that is often the case with Tribal casinos and there is little that can be done about that given the small size of most Tribes and the large families within them. However, this casino was plagued with sibling supervising sibling, "untouchable" disciplinary problems protected by political connections, husbands supervising wives, and a really not-funny problem of the old cliché "they are all in bed together anyway" (in this case literally).

There were employees representing opposing Tribal political factions who held their positions to report to their outside political bosses. There were employees still loyal to former managers and were sending daily revenue reports to those fired managers. Even in the Human Resources department, personal files and background investigations (including my own along with my social security number of ID information) were forwarded to former employees. Vendor kickbacks to employees continued even after David Cook's initial house-cleaning of staff, because the threads of corruption had been sewn so deeply into the fabric of the organization.

My staff and I were offered cash, sex, alcohol, drugs, and gifts to "protect" peoples' jobs, guarantee certain vendor contracts, and look the other way when family of fired employees came into the casino to play games under the control of close friends. The head of the cash drop team was a convicted drug, prostitution, and extortion felon. The head of the cage and vault had pled nolo contendere to charges of embezzling from a national bank. One of the shift managers was a convicted armed robber. The manager of valet parking had been convicted of manslaughter. The number of DUI, drug, and prostitution convicts on the staff was too numerous to keep count.

In addition to the activities I spotted in the OTB and the bar during my walk-through there on the first day, I came to observe a whole menu of unacceptable (if not criminal) behavior that, at very least, was ripping off the Tribe. The beer and wine distributor actually asked me who he should give the cash kickbacks to after I fired one of the bar managers. A player told me that she had come in on a particular day because she had been promised she would win a random drawing if she split payout with the employee conducting the drawing.

One of the bingo managers was loan sharking to a large portion of casino employees. He held titles to their cars, got first dibs on their paychecks, and was running some serious vig on them. A local hardware store manager asked me if he still needed to increase his prices for goods sold to the casino to cover the cash he was required to kickback to casino employees. Several customers asked me if they would still be required to tip departmental managers in order to cash out from a slot machine.

I observed two different employees on two different shifts actually removing money from cash register drawers and putting it in their own pockets; when questioned about it, one denied it and the other admitted that it was routine. Two different women (one married) vying for the position of a department manager's secretary spontaneously (and unsolicited) undressed during his interviews with them. Hand pays from slot machines (bypassing the printed ticket and the accounting system) always increased at night ...until I started requiring management verification of every hand pay.

One of the valet cart drivers (the casino had golf cart pick-up patrons in the parking lot and delivered them to the front door) souped-up the engines in the golf carts and was running (and betting on) drag races nightly between the carts. On one particular night, security cameras recorded two girls removing their shirts and bras and riding on the back of one of the golf carts for over an hour.

In fairness, that sort of outlandish behavior was not so unusual in casino parking lots; one time at the Trump California property we caught a clown (literally a guy we had hired for a party, dressed in a clown costume) having sex on the hood of a car with one of our cocktail waitresses (while he was in full clown costume. I am not sure which of them was stranger.) But clearly the incidents in this valet department were symptomatic of the property-wide problem of each little fiefdom running out of control without policies and procedures or strong management.

And just to top off the lovely image of the staff that I was getting, one of the first rules I had to enforce was that the female members of the staff should not spit their chewing tobacco juices onto the casino floor (most of the males apparently knew better). This, by the way, was a rampant problem at a casino I opened for a Montana Tribe as well.

This litany of over-the-top and out-of-control scams, renegades, Comancharos, game-placement schemes, and con men was absurdly concentrated in that one Oklahoma casino. To this day, more than a decade later, the former Tribal governor and I still discuss how engrained it was.

In a larger and much more alarming sense, while his casino was unusual in the breadth and depth of the pretty crimes, his casino truly was a symptomatic microcosm of the strains on an emerging gaming industry, and not just in Indian country. Clearly, the vigilance and intense scrutiny imposed by Bob Winter and some of those early regulators was not only called for, but essential.

It is no secret that the casino industry, outside of Indian country, has been plagued from its onset with criminal activity; large amounts of cash tend to draw that element. Adding to that already-susceptible landscape is the history of white swindles against Indians and especially Indian enterprises. Together these historical pestilences created a formidable obstacle to the creators of Indian Gaming. In many cases, the problem fueled the anti-Indian and anti-casino forces, giving them "evidence" for their crusades against Tribes. At the very least, such stories empowered racist and paternalistic calls that Indians could not regulate themselves without the guiding hands of white men. (Apparently ignoring that the majority of these crimes were perpetrated by white men and women.)

Addressing the problem from inside Indian country, the National Indian Gaming Association (the trade association born out of the

BIA's National Indian Gaming Task Force) instituted a series of Gaming Commissioner training and certification programs for Tribal Gaming Commissioner, regulators, gaming operators, and Tribal leadership. During the past decade these programs have generated a regulatory environment overseeing Indian Gaming that rivals (and in many cases surpasses) the most stringent Bob-Winter-esque guidelines.

For example, to work in a Las Vegas casino (other than key management) one only needs a "Sheriff's card" certifying there are no warrants or felony convictions; by contrast in most Indian casinos, an employee on any level must subject to a thorough background investigation and ongoing monitoring. In most cases, Indian country casinos are more stringent than commercial casinos when it comes to protection of assets and casino integrity.

It is a modern regulatory environment shaped by those initial gaming commission pioneers, the out-of-control early operations like I found in Oklahoma, and Indian country's general vigilance against centuries of white con-men. Sovereign Indian Tribes were attacked by the same vermin that attacked commercial casinos, plus the addition of historically anti-Indian pestilences; and still their sovereignty has prevailed.

Despite unadulterated assaults by mobsters, petty criminals, and financial flimflammers, Indian country has provided its own vigilance, protection, and reliability surpassing most other jurisdictions. The attacks continue, as they likely always will in the casino industry and against Native Americans. Tribal vigilance also continues to advance, often leading the way for the rest of the gaming industry.

Chapter Eight

The Double-Edged Sword of Regulation

He who tries to determine everything by law will foment crime rather than lessen it.

—Spinoza

There is no doubt that in the early days of Indian Gaming, financing casinos was considered improbable (if not impossible) in light of Bryan v. Itasca County. There was just no known way to secure a loan or an investment; banks were not willing to loan millions of dollars for construction of buildings with no security or for slot machines that might be declared illegal at any moment.

Equally, there is no doubt that viciously devious criminal assaults on casinos are real, recurring, and harder to halt without the vigilance mandated in regulations written by Winter and people like him, rooted out by investigators like David Cook (himself, a Choctaw Tribal member), and shut down by a variety of casino professionals called in to do operational audits.

There is, however, a "flip-side" of the current regulatory structure that is often overlooked in the refreshing relief of saving Tribal assets from the clutches of thieves. The regulatory structures outlined in IGRA (and its attendant 25 C.F.R.) were designed less for assuring the integrity of the operation and more for restricting the sovereignty of the Tribes.

"It is insulting to the Tribe to tell them that they are somehow incapable of determining what is best for themselves," explained Buddy Levy. His commentary reflected a widespread Tribal feeling that the regulatory structure does NOT mandate a Tribe to "have experienced casino regulators and operators share their knowledge, experience, and skills," but instead, paternalistically decrees that

Tribes are incapable of making financial-protection decisions. The law provides forced-direction from politicians who are no more experienced in either gaming or business than Tribal members, but who do have the benefit of being white.

The lawyer's comment echoed Max Osceola earlier sentiment that IGRA did not "give" any special rights to Tribes but restricted them. It also reverberated the sentiments of many white politicians, emphasized as recently as 2014 by U.S. Congressman Paul Gosar of Arizona who referred to Tribes as "wards of the Federal government." A ward, of course, is the legal term for a foster-care child who must have medical and legal decisions made by a "responsible" adult or by the state in place of parents.

That kind of infantization of Indians as childlike wards was first perpetrated by Chief Justice John Marshall's use of the term in that notorious 1831 Cherokee Nation v. State of Georgia decision. It repeatedly has been the terminology to justify seizing land and wielding economic power over Natives. In fact, IGRA itself requires that in order for a Tribe to conduct gaming, the land where the casino is located must be "held in trust" for the Tribe by the United States government. Hence, the fundamental federal requirement for Indian casino gaming is that paternalistic relationship between the government and its frivolous, childlike, wards.

This sort of marginalizing Native Americans is a Tribal sore spot that goes much deeper than official U.S. Government decree. Many Natives feel that the relegation is culturally perpetuated, as well, in characterizations of Indians as frivolous sports-team mascots, a "vanishing race," or "noble savages." In the eyes of many Natives, these cultural categorizations provide the substructure that allows the more overt classification of "wards of the State."

More pointedly to the regulatory double-edged sword, it is certainly worth noting that neither of the extreme examples I cited here were quelled as a result of federal regulations. The Oklahoma casino where the treasurer called me was already under federal regulation and had an NIGC-approved Tribal Gaming Ordinance as well as an active Gaming Commission. Bob Winter's intense scrutiny in writing Internal Control Standards for the Pequot was the direct result of Skip Haywood's insistence on protecting his people and their assets. Even that early investigation in the Seminole's first funding partners was not because of federal regulations, but was because of the Tribe itself.

The reality is that scams against casinos have always existed and scams against Tribes have always existed. The only issue is whether or not Indians are too "childlike" or mascot-esque to make their own decisions and to protect themselves. The historical position of the U.S. government—*as recently as this century with that Arizona Congressman's statement at a public hearing*—has been that only the "great white fathers" were wise enough to make such decisions. In that realm, it is equally noteworthy that there has never been the level of corruption in Indian Gaming anywhere near any of the many notorious Las Vegas scandals from Bugsy Siegel to Lefty Rosenthal.

Beyond the idiotically controlling paternalism, the federal guidelines have other "double-edged" blades. For example, after I "cleaned up" that Oklahoma Tribe's casino, their elected government was voted out of office and replaced by some of the people we had fired in our investigation of corruption. Those officials immediately removed the members of Tribal Gaming Commission and appointed their own operatives to regulate the casino under their terms. Following federal guidelines, the new commissioners fired me and the mangers the previous Tribal Council had brought in; they then revoked our gaming licenses. Eleven years later when I was listed as a board member of a slot machine company, that company was denied a gaming license because of their association with me—a person whose license had been revoked and, under federal guidelines, was a persona non-grata. It ultimately took affidavits from the previous Gaming Commission and Tribal officials to clear the matter and reveal it as a political retaliation against their criminal activities. The absurdity was that the vindictive officials were operating under the guidelines instilled by federal regulations.

Unfortunately, that very personal example is not an isolated incident of revenge. The universe of casino General Managers is littered with high-integrity individuals who ended up on the wrong side of regulatory struggles. I love telling the story of a friend who was befuddled by a Gaming Commission asking, "We see from the record you have had three speeding tickets within the past year; since you clearly do not respect the laws and regulations of the State, why should we believe that you would respect the gaming laws and regulations?"

Beyond paternal requirements and bureaucratic abuses, the regulatory requirements for gaming investments by non-Tribal entities (including banks) has continued to limit the ability of Tribes to enlarge their economic development programs though casino expansion. Even with the legal device of a "limited waiver of sovereign immunity," there are strict federal restrictions on the terms, conditions, and time limits of investments and the financial history of investors. Again, either by design or consequence, the regulatory structure (if not the specific regulations) has effectively placed limits on the Tribe's sovereign right to make their own decisions.

Outside of the inner workings of the industry, from a consumer standpoint, the regulations have carried a double-edge for players as well. While on the one hand, there are requirements for game integrity, there are also mandates that effectively assure scams.

The decreed restrictions on Tribal game types was what gave birth to the entire seeming-absurdity of invisible bingo balls, virtual bingo cards, and cartoon movies representing bingo outcomes: electronic Class II games. Moreover, historically, those Class II games have not paid-out as well as Class III slot machines (though in recent years that has changed as Tribes have assumed more control from the federal government). In short, restricting Tribes from making their own decisions has created deceits against players (even down to those manufacturers chiding me for calling their games "Class II slot machines" rather than "electronic bingo devices."

Discussions among Native American members of the Tribal Regulatory Task Force, the Bingo Task Force, and the BIA's National Indian Gaming Task Force (which eventually became the NIGA trade association for Indian Gaming), have shown that these pioneers of early Indian Gaming regulations were gallant warriors fighting for protection of Tribal sovereignty. The compromises they made were, many times, tradeoffs against even deeper encroachments on sovereignty, and economic development.

From the onset, while there certainly were noble intentions from some of the drafters of the original regulations, it is clear that others authors were intent on—and successful at—limiting the independent and sovereignty of Tribes, apparently with little actual regard for consumers.

Further limiting the absolute sovereignty of Tribes, federal regulations require that in order for a Tribe to offer Class III games, the Tribe must enter into a compact with the state in which they are located. A compact is an official-sounding word for a contract between governments. Typically, a compact not only forces the Tribe to pay a tribute to the state government (in the form of a tax), but also imposes some degree of the state's civil and criminal judicial systems on the Tribe. In other words, compacts normally take away the sovereign governing rights of Tribes to have control over many of their own civil and criminal adjudication.

Consequently, in a seemingly schizophrenic decree, IGRA and its regulations declare that Tribes are "allowed" to have casinos because they are sovereign nations not subject to the civil laws of the state, and at the same time, in order to have full casinos, Tribes must cede to the civil (and criminal) laws of the state. This classic mixed-signal directive of federal law is exactly why Tribal leaders like Max Osceola and Tribal attorneys like Buddy Levy insist that IGRA didn't "give" Tribes anything but does take away even more treaty sovereign rights of Tribes.

The intrusion into a Tribe's right to run their own affairs does not stop with these general decrees. It continues to the level of micro-management of the day-to-day activities of how a Tribe conducts its own business. After defining the three classes of gaming and establishing the requirement that casinos be located on land held in trust for the Ward-Tribe, federal regulations go on to micro-manage the job descriptions of: bingo callers; counting room supervisor; chief of security; custodian of gaming supplies or cash; floor manager; pit boss; dealer; croupier; approver of credit; custodian of gambling devices including slot machines; any other person whose total cash compensation is in excess of $50,000 per year; and, generically, the four most highly compensated persons in the gaming operation.

The micro-management continues by setting requirements for the sovereign nation's emergency preparedness, fire suppression, law enforcement, food and potable water supply, construction and maintenance, sanitation and solid waste, and other infrastructure requirements; all as minimum requirements for the supposedly sovereign Tribe to conduct casino gaming.

In the government-to-government negotiations between Tribes and states for a compact, the Federal regulations impose stringent requirements for the content of those compacts and the final paternal authority of the Department of Interior to disapprove any compact. In other words, the sovereign nation may enter into a contract with the state, but the government of the great white fathers must approve any contract presented by their wards.

The regulations continue their intrusion by requiring federal approval of how casino revenue is used by the Tribe. While specifically stating that the Tribes have the "powers of self-government," the same section of the Code of Federal Regulations requires that net revenue from gaming can only be used "to fund tribal government operations or programs; to provide for the general welfare of the tribe and its members; to promote tribal economic development; to donate to charitable organizations; or to help fund operations of local government agencies." IGRA further requires that it is illegal to make per capita payments to tribal members from net gaming revenues without a Department of Interior approved tribal revenue allocation plan.

These seeming encroachments on the Tribe's ability to self-govern completely (or at least to operate their own business) are hardly a scratch on the surface of the level of federal intervention into the day-to-day management of a Tribal casino. The depths of micro-management of the business enterprises of these ward-nations are truly mind-boggling to the average gambler. The federal minimum internal control standards for gaming operations on Indian land contain specific regulations for: customer database management; hold percentages; ante; betting stations; betting tickets; bill acceptors in slot machines; the canisters that hold the bills inside the machine and even the release process for those canisters; electronic meters inside slot machines; supervisors in crap games; cash cages; player credit; auditing accountability; call bets; card room banks; cash out methods; chips; how the money is counted and who may count it; how cards may be dealt; number, type, functionality, and physical position of cameras; how keys are maintained; the memory chips inside slot machines; pull tab sheets; price structures and pay tables; jackpots; linked electronic games; motion-activated cameras; parimutuel wagering activities; progressive jackpots; card game rakes; the reel symbols on slot machines; employees who transport chips of cash; shift management of casino employees; statistical win of the casino and of the player; inventory of gaming supplies and equipment; weigh scales; how coins are stored; what control rules a Tribe may institute on their own businesses; required CPA audits and what, specifically, the CPA must look for; specific checklist for testing various departmental procedures; the format of internal reporting; and much more.

Such depths of required minimum internal control standards are the most dramatic example of that double-edged sword of regulation. On one hand, these types of regulatory guidelines give an excellent template of how to protect consumers and simultaneously protect the Tribal assets. At the same time, the depth of the micro-management by the federal government is unprecedented; there are no such federal micro-management guidelines for the steel industry, textile mills, department stores, automotive dealerships, or any other private enterprises. Clearly, somewhere along the line, someone did not feel that Indians were capable of managing their own affairs, learning to manage their own businesses, or capable or properly hiring people to work for them (without federal approval).

Chapter Nine

The Management and Development Contract

He who does not trust enough, will not be trusted.

—Lao Tzu

Building off the mythos of the noble but childishly naïve savage mascot in need of protection, the micro-managing tentacles of the federal government's control wrap tightly around even the managers of Indian casinos. Federal law requires U.S. government approval of some of the most minute internal affairs of their subordinate wards; even determining who may be hired to operate a casino, how much they may be paid, and how long they may be employed.

Buddy Levy's brilliantly revolutionary paradigm for financing and operating the Seminole Tribe's foray into gaming would have been completely illegal under the regulations of the Indian Gaming Regulatory Act. Fortunately for the Seminole Tribe, and Indian Gaming nationwide, there was no IGRA when Jim Clare, Buddy Levy, and Pan American Corporation created that management contract model for casino financing and operations.

That model was so effective (and profitable) for the Tribe that even after the passage of IGRA outlawed it, the Seminole Tribe elected to continue with Buddy's original prototype in 1994 when Pan American financed and opened the Tribe's Immokalee Florida casino. When they had run out of money to finish that casino on their own, Chief Billie asked Jim Clare to step in and spend $2.5 million to finish the little building. In return, Pan American operated the property for the next four years.

A full decade earlier, IGRA had decreed a complex obstacle course of management and development of contract prohibitions. Obviously aimed at prohibiting the rapid casino expansion allowed by the Clare-Levy model, IGRA forced the federal position that Indians were

93

incapable of making decisions about their own welfare. Consequently, once federal regulators realized what had happened four years earlier in Immokalee, they fined Pan American $2 million for operating without a federally approved management contract. Approval by a sovereign Tribe was not sufficient under the IGRA guidelines.

"We were so beneficial to the Tribe that Chief Billie and the Council stepped in and paid the fine for us," Levy remembered, noting that to avoid further conflict, his company turned over operations of Immokalee to Tribal managers that had been trained by Levy and Clare.

Before IGRA, the Department of Interior took the position that the U.S. government had no interest or jurisdiction over Indian bingo, gaming, or the management structure. As IGRA began to take shape, the authors began to focus on Buddy's business model. Fueled by a combination of Las Vegas paranoia and an obvious desire to limit outside experts helping gaming expansion, the regulations established complex limits on outside management companies.

Though Buddy's original 20-year contract for Tampa remained "grandfathered in" and free of federal meddling until the dawn of the 21st century, it was clear that IGRA regulations had effectively killed the model and the potential for gaming expansion that it had created.

Assuming a Tribe was incapable of evaluating and vetting management companies, the new regulations defined the responsibilities of management companies in micro-detail and set requirements for complete background investigations of anyone having a financial interest in the contract or owning 10% or more of the stock in a management company. In addition to requiring detailed resumes and references, the law also required a complete financial statement for anyone associated with the company.

Most interestingly, however, these requirements were at the federal level and circumvented any decision the Tribe may have made. Just to demonstrate what head-buzzing the micromanaging circumvention required, here are just a few of the federal requirements:

- An oral interview with all principals of a potential management company to determine each individual's "suitability" to be part of such a company (the guidelines for suitability were totally subjective from the interviewer).
- A compensation limit for the company of no more than 30% of *net* casino revenue (except in special situations).

- Contracts that last no longer than five years.
- Automatic disqualification of companies with any employee, owner, or associate who is a Tribal member.
- Automatic disqualification of companies with any employee, owner, or associate who has been convicted of *any* felony.
- Automatic disqualification of companies with any employee, owner, or associate who has been convicted of a misdemeanor *gambling* offense.
- Automatic disqualification of companies with any employee, owner, or associate who provides false information on the application form.
- Arbitrarily automatic disqualification of companies with any association who *has been determined to be a person whose prior activities... or reputation, habits, and associations pose a threat to the public interest or to the effective regulation and control of gaming....*

Further assuming that Tribes were incapable of the vetting process, IGRA required that potential management companies provide to the federal government the following:

- A list of the largest beneficiaries and trustees when the entity is a trust; or the ten largest partners when the entity is a partnership; or each person who is a director or who is one of the ten largest holders if the issues and outstanding stock alone or in combination with another stockholder who is a spouse, parent, child, siblings (*note the awkward wording of that regulation*).
- Copies of documentation establishing the existence of the entity, such as the partnership agreement, the trust agreement, or the articles of incorporation.
- Copies of documents designating the person who is charged with acting on behalf of the entity.
- Copies of bylaws or other documents that provide the day-to-day operating rules for the entity.
- A description of any previous business relationships with Indian Tribes, including ownership interest in those businesses.
- A description of any previous business relationships with the gaming industry generally, including ownership interest in those businesses.

- The name and address of any licensing or regulatory agency with which the person has filed for a license or permit relating to gaming.
- For each misdemeanor conviction or ongoing misdemeanor prosecution within ten years of the date of the application, the name and address of the court involved, the dates of the prosecution, and of the disposition.
- For each criminal charge regardless of whether or not it resulted in a conviction, if such charge is within 10 years of the date of the application, the name and address of the court involved, the charges and the dates of the charges and of the disposition.
- Complete financial statements for the previous three years.
- A signed Notice Regarding False Statements for each entity.
- Proof of funds showing available operating capital on hand to sustain business.

While this type of documentation is standard due diligence material, scrutiny was taken away from the Tribes' discretion and became federalized. As if these administrative screenings were not enough encroachment on decision-making of a sovereign Tribe, the IGRA requirements continued to actually nit-pick how the management company would operate. Under the guidelines, for management contract authorization, the NIGC must approve the following:

- The operating days and hours the management company is available.
- What provisions the company has for hiring, firing, training, and promoting employees.
- The company's methodology for maintenance of the books and more specifically how financial statements will be prepared.
- How independent auditors will be paid.
- The company's provisions for the hiring and supervision of security personnel.
- The management company's provisions for fire protection services.
- Setting the advertising budget and the company's plans for purchasing advertising.

- The company's proposed procedures for paying bills.
- The company's structure for obtaining and maintaining insurance coverage.
- The company's proposed schedule for reporting to the Tribal Gaming Authority.
- The maximum dollar amount the company expects for the recoupment of development and construction costs.
- The proposed structure for terminating the contract.

The Chairman of the NIGC, not the Tribe itself, must determine if any investment made is "reasonable" for the Tribe. All management contracts are public records and are published by the NIGC. Finally, no management contract is legal until it is approved and signed by the Chairman of the NIGC.

This circumvention of the Tribal decision-making process provides a sufficient barrier to entry to many who would want to invest in or operate an Indian casino. Even for the few willing to navigate the labyrinth, it is virtually assured that there will never be another Levy-esque 20-year management contract that finances new casinos.

Nonetheless, some of the highest profile casino operating companies in America have gone through the IGRA process to obtain very lucrative management contracts at Indian casinos. Caesars Palace has had the management contracts for the Eastern Band of Cherokee Indians in Cherokee, North Carolina, for the Rincon Band of Luiseno Indians in San Diego County, California, as well as four other Tribes. Las Vegas company, Stations Casinos, developed and manages a massive San Francisco Bay area casino for the Federated Indians of Graton Rancheria, and a handful of other Tribal casinos. Though they currently have no Tribal management contracts, casino industry giants Steve Wynn, MGM Resorts, Sun International, and others have flirted with the process.

Despite a history of opposition to Indian casinos, primarily because of competition to his Atlantic City resorts, Donald Trump finally decided "if he can't beat them; join them." In April of 2000, THCR (Trump Hotel Casino Resort) Management Services signed an NIGC-approved development and management contract with the 13-member Twenty-Nine Palms Band of Luiseno Mission Indians in Coachella California. In March of 2002, after a massive

redevelopment of the tiny casino, Trump, personally, signed an
amended version of the contract. It was the first foray into Indian
country for Donald Trump and his gaming empire of three Atlantic
City casinos and one Chicago-area riverboat casino. For the Tribe, it
was their second management and development agreement, having
entered the gaming business under a 1994 NIGC-approved contract
with another developer.

The Trump agreement is almost a template of compliance with the
checklist for contracts provided by the NIGC. The only anomaly in
the mogul's agreement was a monthly licensing fee paid to him for the
use of his name on the casino logos. As part of that licensing, the
property was rebranded from "Spotlight 29" to "Trump 29"; the "29"
was from the Tribe's name and not as Howie Mandel joked in my
showroom there, "not my favorite Trump casino—Trump 28 is nicer;
Trump 17 is not so much." Trump's licensing fee was not part of the
management contract, but was another agreement.

Another unusual, though not unheard of, feature of the Trump
contract was that the Trump employees (myself included) would be paid
from the Tribe's funds and we would all technically be employees of the
Tribe but hired, managed, reporting to, or fired by Trump. This often was,
at very least, a sore spot between the Trump management staff and the
other employees who were direct employees of the Tribe only.

At the time Trump arrived, the Tribe operated the smallest
casino/bingo hall in the Palm Springs—Coachella Valley area of
California; a hall that had opened under the auspices of the earlier
management contract with another company. On behalf of the Tribe,
Trump agreed to syndicate loans for a $60 million expansion to the
casino in exchange for a management fee of 30% of net revenue.
Ultimately, the financing package that he arranged included a personal
loan to the Tribe for $11 million.

The massive redesign did not include either a hotel or a parking garage;
instead, a large R.V. park was designed behind the casino. The floor
changed from a few hundred games, a bingo hall, and a fast-food diner
to a 2,000-machine floor with no bingo hall; a 2,100-seat entertainment
center, booking some of the biggest names in entertainment; a celebrity
chef gourmet restaurant widely recognized as the best in the Palm Springs
area; a food court that included a McDonalds as well as four other
restaurants and a combination buffet dinner; an upscale high-tech

nightclub with live music; a massive table-games pit; a valet-parking porte-cochère; a constant prize-giving players club; two bars; and a series of interior architectural eye-dazzling features—one which Trump claimed to have personally designed (and he may have).

During the second bankruptcy of the Trump gaming empire, our Trump 29 casino remained both profitable and the single shining star of his casino demesne. His commercial empire was almost $2 billion in debt, but Trump 29 was profitably paying him millions. When he visited the casino in 2004, amid a press swarm surrounding the first season of "The Apprentice," Trump was briefly caught off-guard when a reporter blurted out a question comparing the casino's finances to his Atlantic City properties.

Revealing, at least to me, what a professional performer he is, instinctively Trump undetectably leaned an ear toward me to hear me whisper to him the answer to the reporter's question. In a brilliant flash of showmanship, he immediately launched into the hyperbole and superlatives that have always been his trademark. "We are THE MOST successful casino in California. We are doing better than anything in Atlantic City, Las Vegas, or anywhere in the world," he responded to the reporter's question.

In a private meeting later that day with 12 of the 13 Tribal members, Trump was confronted with an entirely different kind of challenge. Though the revenue had more than doubled in the past year, the Tribe had become disenchanted with the Trump charm and his company's failure to deliver many of the over-the-top promises made during the original presentation to them. The Tribe had also come to feel that since they were paying the salaries of his employees, they did not need Donald Trump to hire professional casino operators. Those grievances plus Trump's own failure to show up very frequently combined to inspired at least one Tribal Council member to wear (mimicking the catch-phrase from his hit television show).

Though the NIGC-approved management contract was effectively "iron-clad," it did contain an "out clause" should THCR file bankruptcy or become insolvent. Trump's 2004 bankruptcy of Trump Hotels and Casinos Resorts' $1.8 billion debt (the third of his four corporate bankruptcies) resulted in his stake in the company being reduced to only 27% and opened that door for the Tribe to "fire" him.

Trump set up THCR in 1995 as a publically traded company created for a series of high-finance bank-account shuffles. The company started with the Trump Plaza, at the center point of the Atlantic City boardwalk, as its single asset. The then-under-development Chicagoland riverboat (in Gary, Indiana) was in the portfolio as a projected asset. The next year, the company bought the Taj Mahal from Trump personally, paying him $890 million. THCR also bought the Trump Castle for $486 million, including $355 million in debt assumption. The same year, the Castle was renamed "Trump Marina" and the company announced a new boardwalk casino called "Trump World's Fair" (which the company operated for three years). In 1999 THCR signed an agreement to purchase the Flamingo Hilton casino in Kansas City for $15 million, but Missouri gaming regulators did not approve the license application and that purchase died. In 2000, the Coachella deal was signed.

In October of 2004, a refinance deal with Credit Suisse was rejected by Trump's bondholders; so later that month the tycoon hired Morgan Stanley to create a $500 million restructuring plan which was accepted by U.S. Bankruptcy Court in December. The same year, he changed the company's name to Trump Hotels and Casino Resorts.

Despite allegations raised during President Trump's 2016 campaign that he had somehow failed as a casino operator, it is noteworthy that the bankruptcies were all related to banking and bondholder issues rather than operations. Reality is that in both commercial and Indian casinos the organization that Donald Trump put together was among the most effective and successful ever assembled in the gaming industry. Trump was in fact a brilliant marketer and casino operator who was in constant battle with bankers and bondholders.

All of this maneuvering opened the NIGC contract clause that would allow the Twenty-Nine Palms Band of Mission Indians to cancel the contract, or at least to buy it out. Recognizing that casino as his one cash-cow, Trump was reluctant to give up the lucrative agreement. On the advice of legal counsel, the Tribe responded with an IGRA-allowed double-edged sword of regulation: they instructed their Tribal Gaming Commission to revoke Trump's gaming license. Besides ending the California relationship, such an action could cause the New Jersey Gaming Control Commission to revoke his license in that jurisdiction; licensing revocation in one jurisdiction usually has a snowball effect, regardless of the reason for the revocation.

To represent him against the Tribe, their lawyer, and their Gaming Commission, Trump hired well-known gaming lawyer Dennis Whittlesey to work alongside his in-house team of lawyers. More than a decade later, at the cocktail party for the *International Masters of Gaming Law*, Whittlesey still had a slight cringe as he recalled those grueling negotiations.

"The Tribe really wanted to get rid of him," Whittlesey recalled. The buy-out for the contract was $11 million, but as Whittlesey recalled, the Tribe had no interest in paying that. Whittlesey was finally able to negotiate a $6 million fee for Trump to walk away. His biggest concern was selling that deal to Donald J. Trump. Whittlesey amusingly remembered Trump's in-house lawyer on the phone with "The Donald" and Whittlesey hearing "Dennis will explain the deal to you." To his surprise, Trump only asked a couple of simple questions and then agreed.

Whittlesey also recalled how unyielding the Tribe's attorney had been in his adamancy to revoke the Trump license. That same attorney had furiously threatened my license two weeks earlier, apparently enraged that my resignation had been to Trump and not to the Tribe itself. Whittlesey, with a tone of irony in his voice, reminded me that the same attorney was later convicted and sentenced to two years in Federal prison after pleading guilty to conspiracy to commit bribery in a construction kickbacks scheme to a company he owned and assigned Tribal business.

Meanwhile, the Trump contract with the Tribe remains a model of what needs to be included in an agreement to obtain NIGC approval under the IGRA guidelines. Like all NIGC-approved contracts, THCR's is public record, published by the NIGC and redacting only the specifics of the financial arrangements between the parties. To illustrate that template, and its complexity, I have included the full, albeit redacted, text of that Trump contract in the Appendix of this book. Since Donald Trump has become President of the United States, this public-record contract becomes even more historically interesting both for its model for Indian casino management contracts as well as for insight into the businesses of the President.

Despite the attempts of IGRA's authors to complete quash the Clare-Levy model, management contracts are still a viable and common practice in Indian gaming. Moreover, just as modern minds responded to IGRA's Class II universe with virtual bingo cards, invisible ball drops, and movie representations of bingo outcomes, out-of-the-box thinkers found alternatives to the IGRA management contract parameters as well.

Former National Indian Gaming Commissioner Dan Little told me, in 2016, "More and more we were seeing *management consulting agreements* trying to get around the Management Contract scrutiny."

To avoid the barriers to entry, the 30% compensation limit, the maximum five-year term, and what one developer called "the Federal Government crawling up my ass with a flashlight," many operators have become "management consultants." In any number of variations of that term, the developer/manager takes the NIGC management contract checklist and writes a consulting contract that serves the same purpose (financing in exchange for a percentage of revenue and control of the operation) without any of the triggers that would have the agreement fall under the jurisdiction of the NIGC's management regulations.

This sort of tenuous gray area is, in many cases, the only way some high-risk Tribes can obtain financing and professional management; at least until they reach a point where they are successful and profitable.

Chapter Ten

Just How Much Money ARE We Talking About, Here?

The big money is made by taking risks.

—Bernard Madoff

There is something about Tribal casinos that brings out the likes of Donald Trump, Chinese billionaire Lim Goh Tong, Vegas mogul Steve Wynn, and the ire of anti-Indian forces who still argue that Tribes are "wards of the government." Chances are it's the money, or at least the perception of the money.

For the small to mid-sized Tribal casinos that I have operated, it has not been unusual to generate more than $100 million a month in *gross revenue*. A Tribal mega-casino resort could typically generate a half-billion dollars a month. That is, $1.2 billion and $6 billion annually, respectively.

Only about 15% of the revenue goes to direct operational expenses (direct labor, food, bingo supplies, etc.), leaving the Tribe 85% to pay indirect operating expenses (advertising, general and administrative costs, and so on). Net profit at Tribal casinos typically hovers around 25% of revenue (historically higher than commercial casinos, probably because there is less Wall Street style "monkey business" going on with the finances of a Tribally owned casino).

That is a lot of money and this is a very formulaic business. It is also a very specialized business with very specialized metrics and business terminologies that have entirely different meanings than they do in traditional business and finance.

For example, in almost every business, the term "gross revenue" means the amount of money customers actually pay to make their purchases. It does not include cost of goods nor operating costs; it simply is what the customer pays. It is real cash money and must be handled, counted, audited, and tracked.

Similarly, in a casino, the monthly $100 million (that I cited) is the total amount of money spent by customers—*wagered*. Like all gross revenue, it is real cash money that must be handled, counted, audited, and tracked. However, those "purchases" are the amounts *wagered* in slot machines; 91.5% of that money is paid out in winnings and jackpots to players.

After those payouts to winners, the casino is left with only 8.5%; only $8.5 million of that $100 million that I cited. In the casino world, *gross revenue* is NOT total expenditures by customers, rather, *casino gross revenue* is the amount of "sales" minus the amount of "payouts."

While, on the surface, this might seem like merely a matter of semantics, closer attention reveals that this equivocation of terminology is indicative of the complex special metrics necessary to understand casino profits.

With specialized metrics, one has to wonder: "What return on investment should outside investors or management companies expect? How does an Indian casino measure success? How profitable can (or should) a Tribal casino be? How much debt can a casino realistically service?"

According to the U.S. Securities and Exchange Commission, in 2002 Donald Trump's management contract in Coachella for *30%-of-net* earned him $2.7 million; in 2003 it earned $3.2million. Late that year he hired me as Vice President of Marketing and Player Development and in 2004 he made $7.5 million; almost two and a half times what he had walked away with before I took over.

Those numbers represent 30% of casino EBITDA (*Earnings Before Interest, Taxes, Depreciation and Amortization*) plus the fee to license his name to the casino. In 2004, according to the SEC, our casino's EBITDA was around $25 million. By the following year, the 13-member Tribe had fired Trump and bought out the remaining years of his contract for the mere $6 million that Dennis Whittlesey had negotiated; an amount Trump apparently needed since his commercial casinos were in their third bankruptcy by then.

All of that raises two more questions: "What are the metrics for expenses of an Indian casino?" and "what is the structure for a modern investment deal in an Indian casino?"

Investor deals for Indian casinos can include direct loans or syndicated loans at market rate financing PLUS 25% to 35% of gross slot machine revenue PLUS 30% of net revenue for the management contract. Hence, for the investor, a 60-month financing deal could mean an insane-sounding 400% return on investment.

In Donald Trump's case, he syndicated $49 million of the $60 million loaned to the Twenty-nine Palms Band, using only $11 million dollars of his own money. For that $11 million, he was paid a total of $19.4 million (the three operational years plus the buyout fee). That is, roughly, a 57% return on investment.

Even further indicative of how out-of-sync Tribal casino metrics are with the "real" world, that 57% return is widely considered a massive failure by Trump. In the context of these investments, if 400% R.O.I. is feasible, then a "mere" 57% could be considered a failure. In any other world, that large of a return would be an amazing success.

In 2016, during Trump's presidential campaign, the Palm Springs newspaper interviewed my friend Victor Rocha about that investment. Victor, a member of Pechanga Band of Luiseño Indians, is the creator and owner of the most influential daily news source about Indian Gaming, Pechanga.net. In the interview he said, "When Trump came in, we all thought, 'Oh gosh, he is going to really run the tables on the tribe,' and it was actually just the opposite that happened. But it shouldn't have been a surprise. If you look at anything that guy has done in this industry, he has a lead thumb—it's the opposite of a golden touch."

Again, the fact it is considered a "lead thumb" failure to have a 57% return on invest in only three years is very revealing about the nature of the industry. The average annual return on investment of the Dow Jones Industrial Average is 8.8% a year; 26.4% over three years. Trump doubled that and he is considered an abject failure! More interestingly, Victor was absolutely right in his assessment; the Trump investment was a comparative failure. A more prudent Indian Gaming investment group would have been closer to the 400% than the 57%. Despite the Indian country metric, Trump's investment was an incredible success by Wall Street standards for a "normal" business. So depending on one's seat, Trump could have been either a massive failure or a business-genius success.

Wells Fargo Bank has an entire division that focuses exclusively on the $2 billion-plus annual financing of Native American gambling halls; and they handle about 50% of that business. Bank of America followed the Wells Fargo lead and has captured 40% of the market, leaving between 8% and 9% of the market to the new Indian Gaming divisions of CIT Group, Key, Morgan Stanley, and other "usual suspect" institutional investors. The industry's remaining 1% to 2% is left to smaller funds, investment companies, and individual investors.

To understand the revenue of an Indian casino (or any casino, for that matter), and how little of that revenue the Tribe actually receives, one needs to understand how to measure casino success. One needs to understand those specialized metrics and the specialized challenges presented by those metrics.

A well-marketed mid-sized casino might have $5 million a day passing through its count room, though $4.6 million of that typically is paid back in cash to winning players. As noted, casinos have a daily cash-flow that is far beyond the parameters of any typical small business paradigm. All of that cash not only serves as bait to the unsavory, but also requires specialized analytics and tracking; not complicated, but definitely specialized.

In fact, the U.S. Treasury Department requires casinos to report large cash transactions to the Financial Crimes Enforcement Network (FinCEN) of the IRS, as part of "Title 31" (the Bank Secrecy Act). Originally written for banks only, Title 31 training is now required for all casino employees who come in contact with cash; casino cashier cages serve many consumer banking functions. Concerns over laundering of drug money, terrorist evasion of international money-transfer standards, and gamblers' petty tax-evasion scams caused the IRS to extend the audit and reporting requirements to casinos.

Amid that landscape of paranoia over the vast amounts of cash, the primary metric for measuring casino revenue is what we call "win-per-unit-per-day" (wpupd); a number determined by the amount of money wagered in a slot machine minus the payouts to winning players. For the casino's math, the "win" is how much the casino wins, not the player. This is the casino version of the gross revenue. Nationwide in Indian casinos, the average slot machine wpupd is 8.5% of the amount wagered; meaning that for every $100 put into a slot machine, the casino keeps $8.50 and pays out $91.50 back to players.

Some casino operators and some Tribes view every revenue center at the property as its own profit and loss accounting center. In those cases, if the casino department gives a free dinner to a high-roller customer, then the casino gets a bill from the restaurant.

Looking at overall casino revenue, about 88% of *all* revenue comes from slot machines—which in turn only takes about 2% of operating expenses. Food and beverage operations generate around 5% of the total revenue of the property; table games account another 2%; entertainment venues generate about 1.5% of overall revenue with shopping generating another 1.2%. Hotel revenue accounts for only about half of 1% of the entire revenue picture. Poker rake contributes a little less than 4/10th of 1% with bingo halls bringing in about 1/3rd of 1% of the overall revenue.

Other operators, myself included, think that it is a silly model to take money out of one pocket and put it another pocket of the same suit. Instead, I base all operating expenses of every department of the property on the primary revenue source of the property: the slot machines. I operate toward the goal of "break-even" (rather than profit) for all other units (food and beverage, table games, entertainment, shopping, hotel, poker, bingo, etc.). If there is measurable profit from any of those units, I view it as "icing on the cake" of the primary business unit of slot machines. If those departments have zero profit, I really don't care as long as the customers continue to play the slot machines and the other departments operate within my budgeted parameters.

Both business models require the same sort of micro-analysis of each department's operating expenses and revenue. The fundamental difference is focus of resources. My model focuses on gambling, the slot machines specifically, while the previous model focuses on making each department profitable.

Using my management methodology, a casino operated with average skills, from that 8.5% gross profit, it typically costs about 51% of the profit to operate the entire property. That number includes labor, supplies, and all operating expenses. It includes utilities and the normal costs of doing business, but does not include slot machine acquisition, property debt service, and related fees; and, of course, it does not include management and development fees.

If the slot machines were not purchased (as part of initial CAPEX), then in addition to the 51%, there is another 27.5% to pay for leasing slot machines. Typically, a generic slot machine leases for 20% of the wpupd, while a "premium" slot machine title leases for 35%; so 27.5% is an average. Premium games and Class II games are almost never available for purchase; and even purchased games have daily maintenance and upgrade fees.

Class II games are, as discussed earlier, tax exempt. Taxes on Class III games are usually a percentage of the wpupd. That percentage varies by state compact and the range is everywhere from 4% to 50%; but an average (not a median) is around 10% tax on machine revenue after payouts.

So, from the wpupd, 88.5% is immediately committed to operations, games acquisition, and taxes. From the remaining 11.5% of the wpupd, a typical management contract will cost the Tribe 30% of that net, leaving the Tribe a little more than 8% of wpupd. Debt service and other fess must be paid from that remainder, often as much as 65% of that number. The Tribe then has whatever is left, typically about 3% of the wpupd.

Converting these percentages to real numbers, across Indian country and excluding the mega-resorts, an average slot machine takes in about $3,500 per day in play. The machine typically pays back around $3,202 of that, leaving the casino about $297 a day per machine. After the expense percentages listed above, a typical Tribal casino is left with about $8.91 per slot machine per day. Multiply that by 1,500 slot machines and the slot-machine profit for a casino should be around $13,365 a day or $406,518 a month and $4.8 million a year net–net. That $4.8 million is then used of social programs or distribution of profits to members.

A casino can take in almost $2 billion a year in actual cash wagers and end up with a final profit of about one-quarter-of-one-percent of that cash flow. That is why special cash handling procedures are in place and why special metrics are used to measure success. This is also why investors, banks, gangsters, and government watchdogs are all so interested in that other 99.75% of the revenue; it is a big number.

Every year dozens, if not scores, of non-Indian want-to-be investors approach me about Indian Gaming "deals" they have supposedly found. At the same time, I am pitched an equal number of casino projects by "non-recognized" Tribes or individuals identifying themselves as Natives but without Tribal support.

The first question I always ask is the same question that Don Corleone asked Virgil Sollozzo in the original Godfather film: *Why do you come to me? Why do I deserve your generosity?* If a legitimate deal is going to bring the investor tens (or hundreds) of millions of dollars' profit, then why is it not on the plate of Wells Fargo or one of the other big boys?

While investment banks certainly have the appetite for those preposterously high revenue-sharing returns in addition to payment on the principle and interest... most do not have the same voracious hunger for the risk level associated with most Indian casino finance deals—at least not without a guarantor/underwriter. Even fewer have the taste for the intense management required to secure such returns.

The biggest hurdle to obtaining these loans is the lack of collateral that comes with sovereignty. Going all the way back to the "Bryan" decision and earlier, fee-simple control is illegal for a lender to Indian Tribes; and that is just the most obvious hurdle. Interestingly enough, only about 45% of eligible Tribes have casinos, and those eligible Tribes make up less than half of the Tribes that are *potentially* eligible. The prospective market for investment is huge; but so is the risk when getting involved with unrecognized Tribes or land that is not in Trust. Like the returns, the risks are huge.

Following Trump's model, a relatively small investor often can underwrite or guarantee a syndication in exchange for a disproportionately large return in comparison to the overall investment. This is especially true when the syndication is structured as a portfolio loan from a commercial bank. A proportionately small investor with a higher risk tolerance often can obtain majority or near-majority interest in a well-vetted project—especially in some cases, even before the land is approved or before a tribe is "recognized" as eligible.

Focusing on these unusual metrics, an Indian casino loan characteristically is based on casino cash flow rather than LTV (loan-to-value ratios). These loans generally cost more than typical portfolio loans, and they often have seemingly mountainous barriers to investor entry. Consequently, unlike commercial casinos, a typical Indian casino loan is no more than two to three times projected net income, at 3% to 4% above LIBOR (the London Interbank Offered Rate), for five to seven years, amortizing between 35% and 50% of funded amount.

The financing creativity gestated by the cash-flow model and the unavailability of land collateral actually allow for unparalleled flexibility for structuring investments. An almost cafeteria-style assortment of creative possibilities can be assembled to suit the risk tolerance, the investment goals, available capital, and desired active or passive participation of the investor.

As I vet a potential project, I look for a six-point "holy grail" for easy financing:

Is the Tribe Federally recognized?

Does the Tribe have gaming experience?

Is the land in Trust?

Has a feasibility study been conducted for the project?

What is the projected wpupd?

Is there a State compact already in place?

The answers to these six questions determine the most sought-after Indian Gaming investments. Finding the right combination of answers is a rare treasure for an investor who is not one of the "big boys" of banking. The majority of non-banking deals offered are not "holy grail" deals and require intense risk analysis vetting. The structures to put deals together that generate that nirvana 400% R.O.I. versus the failure of "only" 57%, are as complicated as the metrics of the revenue.

The most basic investment in Indian gaming is the model matured by Wells Fargo and the other investment banks. This model is a simple, passive loan. These are term loans, usually five to seven years (though there are no statutory restrictions on term). They typically are offered at two to three times projected net income. As an example, for a proposed casino with a feasibility study projecting 1,500 slot machines with a wpu of $250 per day, the projected annual net revenue is $67 million (based on $136.8 gross revenue). A three-times multiple of that makes the Tribe eligible for a loan of $201 million to build their casino.

That basic loan would be financed at 3% to 4% above LIBOR at the time of closing. Repayment can be full amount at term or a balloon payment with a refinance option after up to seven years. It is not uncommon to charge rates as high as 12%–15% for the money for non "holy grail" deals. These are typically amortized loans, between 25% and 50% annually.

This most simple finance model is the entirety of the deal most frequently embraced by the investment banks, though all of the investment banks have a financial threshold for syndicating the loan. Wells Fargo, for example, will typically direct-lend up to $50 million and lead syndicate the remainder (if there is one).

Key Bank, as another example, has financed deals as small as $8 million as the sole lender and in addition to syndication, also offers high-yield bond financing in terms up to 15 years. In this model, bond money with no recall provisions is often used for the higher risk deals. The advantages to this type of funding is a longer repayment period than traditional bank term money.

Another common finance technique is one that I have used when there were issues keeping banks from getting involved or when I needed another layer of financing, over and above bank financing (which allows for a lower loan principle through this carve-out). In this model, the investor buys slot machines and then leases them to the casino for a percentage of the revenue that over the term of the lease repays the equivalent of expanded multiples of traditional loan P & I payments.

Indian casinos obtain slot machines one of two ways: either through a direct purchase or through a modified lease agreement that I discussed earlier. While lease agreements may be cloaked as "lease-purchase," as "bucket purchase," as "revenue share," as "flat fee lease," and any number of palatable euphemisms, the structures of typical slot machine leases are the same. The lessor collects (a standard) 20% of win per unit for a (federally regulated) term of less than seven years; (in practice many are for 6 years, 11 months, and 29 days).

In the late 1990s in Oklahoma, several Tribes pioneered a methodology for financing casinos by having a slot machine manufacturer pay for the new casino and give it as a gift to the Tribe… in exchange for guaranteed floor space for slot machines for the just-under-seven-year period at up to 35% of wpu rather than the standard 20%.

To visualize this model, let's consider a fictional casino with 1,500 machines and a wpupd of $250. The purchase price of a new slot machine is around $18,000, or $27 million for 1,500 in this example. This allows a gross lease profit of $308 million for the slot machine vendor. If we assume the cost of the casino to be $100 million, then the investor realizes a gross profit of $208 million during the seven-year term. This, of course, is an example only and does not take into account dozens of possible variables, but the model is absolutely valid and has often been used to fund casinos.

A popular variation of this model is for the investor to "buy" floor space inside the proposed casino and place machines in the "purchased" (or, more accurately, "leased") space. This variation frees the investor and the Tribe from the federally mandated limitation of a machine lease of less than seven years; by switching the transaction from a machine lease by the Tribe to the Tribe leasing space to investor, the nature of the transaction is changed (though the percentages remain the same). In either iteration, the model has generated R.O.I. far above the standard bank loan P & I model.

Another finance model has been the Trump-esque fee income structure. Management and Development contracts offer the Tribe expertise and/or generate very lucrative investor fees over and above the financing package. In fact, these fees can be so lucrative that they are often folded into the financing structure. In these modes, the investment group manages the third-party financing on behalf of the Tribe (in whose name the financing remains). Further, the investor group develops the casino for a fee of 4% to 5% of the total cash. Additionally, there is the opportunity to manage for seven years at 25% to 30% of net revenue.

One highly profitable but very simple add-on to any financing package was created in the commercial casino space and exported to Indian country. The model simply adds various development fees and pre-opening management consulting fees to the loan as front-end fees. These additional fees become part of the loan principle or financing package to be repaid by the Tribe over the term of the agreement. These numbers are, customarily, around 8% of the principle and, like a management contract, provide for a nice "sweetener" to the deal structure. This, too, is a Trump-used model.

These finance models, or some combination of them, are the most common practices for arranging financing for Indian casinos, with the latter structure being the standard practice for obtaining large fee incomes in Indian casinos. These structures can further be enhanced with less investment by becoming the underwriter for a lead bank, which is what Trump did with his $11 million.

These models can generate even higher return by investing in pre-land-in-trust projects (after a thorough vetting of special circumstances and conditions) and even pre-recognition projects (provided the likelihood is vetted properly). It is at very least noteworthy that the massively successful Seminole Hard Rock Casino in Tampa Florida—one of the highest revenue generators in the country—began for Buddy Levy and Jim Clare as a pre-land-in-trust speculation.

Chapter Eleven

How I killed Elvis, Attempted to Overthrow the Government, and Made Money for Every Tribal Member

Hell, we don't have to worry about genocide from your people anymore. We Indians are going to kill ourselves off before you have a chance to do anything else to us. Since we have casinos and a little money, white people can just sit back and watch us destroy each other over this bullshit.
—Russell B. Ellis, former Treasurer of Absentee Shawnee Tribe

In Indian country, I killed Elvis. I pissed off almost all of those Class II "slot machine" companies. I "conspired" with the FBI to destroy a casino-finance plan. I raised one Tribe's revenue by $55 million dollars for the sole purpose of seeing my name in print. Oh, and I screwed an oxycodone addict out of a $2 million job at a casino. At least those are among the most common rumors, stories, legends, and complaints about me.

The London Daily Mirror's front-page story announced a parachuting accident in Browning Montana with the headline, *Elvis Breaks His Pelvis*. Mimicking the Las Vegas hotel signs that used to proclaim, *Elvis Slept Here*, I changed the marquis in front of Glacier Peaks Casino to proclaim, *Elvis Crashed Here*. The syndicated television show, *Entertainment Tonight*, led their evening broadcast with my very-edited video of the accident. Even the footage on YouTube doesn't show it all, even with the ambulances in that video.

Unfortunately, The Mirror, my marquis, and the lead story on Entertainment Tonight were not the whole story. My parachuting

Elvis impersonator had died in the casino's parking lot, hitting the ground at almost a mile-a-minute. It appears that I was responsible for the death of Elvis, during an Indian casino grand opening.

Despite the Piegan Blackfeet Nation's strong recent history of economic development projects, the opening of Glacier Peaks Casino was their most ambitious and aggressive project. For that grand opening, I hired the legendary Flying Elvi (also known as the Flying Elvises) a team of precision paratroopers dressed as Elvis impersonators, born from the film *Honeymoon in Vegas*. Since the movie, the Elvis paratroopers had become famous for hundreds of appearances nationwide, including television spots on American Journal; Anthony Bourdain "No Reservations"; Best Damn Sports Show; British Broadcasting Corporation; CNN News; Current Affair; Dinner & A Movie; Donny & Marie; "E" Entertainment; ESPN; Fox Family Channel Promo; Fox FC Channel Promo; Good Morning America; Hard Copy; History Channel; Hoosier Lottery Commercial; Inside Edition; Jerry Lewis MDA Telethon; Nickelodeon; Real TV; Regis Live; The World (Japan's 31 Game Show); Travel Channel; Weddings Of A Lifetime; and many others. Such a dazzling display of Vegas hokeyness was exactly the kind of start I needed to announce to the great Northwest that neon lights had arrived to compete with aurora borealis.

Even by the accounts of those opposed to the strategy and some anti-Indian conservative press, the grand opening was huge. The one-street town was lined with more-thousands of people than the casino could hold or the town of Browning had ever seen. The flying Elvi thrilled the masses by jumping from a plane and soaring over the heads of the crowd to land in the casino parking lot.

Then, in the midst of the grandiose spectacle, the music was cut and the happy-go-lucky MC stopped his banter as one of the dozen parachuting Elvis impersonators, Paul Moran, came in too fast and hit the pavement at almost 60 mph. Moran was a Stockton California building contractor with a passion for water skiing, snowboarding, and unfortunately, sky-diving. News and amateur videos on the Internet showed Moran crashing into the pavement on his right hip and immediately buckling with his head hitting the pavement as his Elvis wig/helmet bounced across the parking lot and his green glider-parachute fell over him like a too-foreboding shroud. The wig/helmet probably prevented a concussion, but the impact crushed his heel and broke his leg. More dangerously, a sharp broken bone fragment sliced his femoral artery and his body began filling with internal bleeding.

Other than an Indian health clinic, the practically inaccessible town of Browning had no medical facilities and no place to land a plane to fly Moran to a full service hospital. Transferred by ambulance to an airport two hours away, and then flown to Harborview Medical Center in Seattle, the flying Elvis died from the injuries.

Meanwhile, the national media made light of the tragic story announcing (in hundreds of newspapers and on television) "Elvis broke his Pelvis" and overlooking the heartbreakingly tragic death. Every editor in each outlet thought that he or she was amazingly original and clever in penning the phrase...which was cliché-mimicked hundreds if not thousands of times by other "creative thinkers."

I, of course in full-spin mode, did not announce his death and gave comments saying that he was taken to the Indian health clinic (which was initially true) and was expected to recover just fine. My spin was supported by television interviews with the founder of the troupe announcing, "He will be back; nothing can keep him out of the sky."

Our spin-control announcements, unfortunately, only contributed to the media's comfort level of making light of the whole tragic affair. The Associated Press as well as several of the national television sensationalist magazine shows turned the entire affair into lighthearted Elvis story that also served as publicity for the casino. In fact, as we watched the next day's national coverage we were disappointed that some of the stories only said "a casino" rather than using the casino name and location. I put my Atlantic City-based press agent to work correcting that oversight; by-god I used to work for Donald Trump and we believe that ALL media is GOOD media! I wanted our name in those stories.

Our reveling in this tragically generated publicity circus actually illustrated the depth of a widespread problem for many Indian casinos, inaccessibility. The *Field of Dreams* "Build it and they shall come," is just not an accurate business model. For each huge success story, like the Seminole Tribe of Florida, Chickasaw Nation, the Mashantucket Pequot Tribe, or the Sycuan Band of the Kumeyaay Nation, there are probably scores of stories of struggling near-failure Indian casino developments.

As recently as 2016, I advised one of those fully eligible Tribes to forget entering into the gaming world and focus their economic development goals on projects other than a casino. Despite their qualifying in all six of my "holy grail" points, their trust-land was just too inaccessible to operate a casino that would serve any constituency other than the 78 people who lived on the Tribal Rancheria. Building serviceable highway access to the trust-land would have costs hundreds of millions of dollars and years to get environmental approvals. Even with my Felix-like bag of tricks for obtaining financing, there was just no viable path to return-on-investment in an acceptable lifetime. Unfortunately, their situation is not as isolated as their land, *most* eligible Tribes share that problem.

Artist John Gast's allegorical Brobdingnagian-like "Miss Columbia," leading settlers across the North American continent, romanticized the American government's manifest destiny that was to Natives the most barbaric of the American atrocities. Part of the barbarism was that forced removal of people from their homelands and relocation to reservations or whatever palatable euphemism we have for internment camps, concentration camps, or involuntary exile. For most of white America, the best known of these atrocities is the infamous Jacksonian Trail of Tears marching Natives to Oklahoma. There are, however, voluminous tragic round-ups of American Indians that rival the Trail of Tears for inhuman brutality.

High on that reprehensible list of ignoble policies is the brutality against the Blackfeet people. The once-feared mighty Algonquin warriors of the plains (from the Great Lakes to the Northern Rockies) were rounded up by the U.S. Army and regulated to the slopes of what is now Glacier National Park—some of the harshest geographies in the continental United States. Clearly, someone in the Department of War wanted to punish these legendary fighters even more than they had done with the alleged (true or false) distribution of smallpox-laced blankets deliberately distributed to the Tribe to wipe out at least half of the population.

I arrived on the Reservation to find a just-started construction project at the end of a 22-mile-long dirt and gravel road. The casino was to be located on the northern realm of Glacier National Park, northeast of the town of East Glacier—more than 50 miles from the closet four-lane highway; 60 miles from an Interstate Highway;

two-and-a-half hours from the closest airport or even a Wal-Mart. Other than the gravel road through open range, the one paved highway south was closed for several months every year due to snowfall; it actually had permanent road-blocking gates that were closed during those months.

The million-and-a-half acres of reservation land was populated by 8,600 people, but there were only 360 households and 254 families in the town. The annual per capita income was about $8,900 and 30% of the town was below the federal "poverty level." During the winter months the sun rose around 10 a.m. and set as early as 2:30 p.m. On some evenings, I could see the aurora borealis. The "Rez" (short for "reservation") town of Browning, itself, is 30 miles northwest of the coldest spot ever recorded in the continental United States and during the one December (of the total 10 months) that I spent there, the warmest day I experienced was -11° (minus eleven degrees) below zero.

The nearby town of Cut Bank holds the world's record for the largest temperature drop in one day: from +44° down to -56 ° in a 24-hour period. "White outs" are common occurrences during much of the year (a terrifying high-wind situation where no objects cast shadows, the horizon is not visible, only dark objects are discernible, and visibility is no more than a few inches). Most cars are equipped with electric block heaters (because the viscosity of motor oil cannot hold without being heated), as well as a glove-compartment stash of chocolate, matches, candles, and space blankets (for the expected (not "possible" but rather "probable") stranded times. Winds, trapped in the mountains, can reach hurricane force with little or no warning. And with global warming, the area has recently been victim of uncontrolled wildfires and flash flooding.

Yes, the American government definitely punished these warriors; but their situation was not unique. Such harsh climates are typical of many Indian reservations around the country. Tribes were forced to locate on callous, uninhabitable lands that white settlers did not want or could not tame. Such was clearly the case with the once warlords of the plains, the Blackfeet Nation. They must have really pissed off someone to be sent to such a place.

According to the American Indian Studies Program at the University of Arizona, this town, Browning Montana, of only

360 households sees at least 50–60 street drunks present every day and alcoholism there is twelve times the national average—in one way or another affecting 100% of the population. The regional Budweiser distributor told me that one convenience store/gas station in town sells more beer in a month than any five other sales outlets combined anywhere in the State of Montana. Following large holiday celebrations, I have witnessed the main street through town littered with beer cans more than a foot-deep along the curbs.

I will spare readers any more of my pent-up lectures on the tragedy of Native Americans and how white abuse, degradation, exploitation, piracy, and attempted genocide have forced the quality-of-life to this stage of unraveling and deconstruction. Less than a melodramatic calamity, the physical situation and the mental state of the people in the situation are byproducts of the last two centuries of white American expansionism. Even more sadly, and painfully, this has manifest in hostility, anger, prejudices, and despair. Combined with the genetic predisposition to alcoholism, the behavior and living standards are disastrous.

Against that less-than-charming, if not tragic, backdrop, I was hired to supervise the completion of construction, hire and train staff, outfit the casino, and get it open. The project was under the auspices of a national-award-winning Tribal business committee, but nonetheless was wrought with an amazing jumble of incompetence, lack of planning, and apparent desperation to get funding.

With an apparent long history of problems with project loans, the business committee was required to find a co-signer or underwriter for the loan to build the new casino. This was not an unusual requirement for Tribes with little or bad credit history. In fact, there is an entire cottage industry of underwriting syndicated loan guarantees for tribes (in exchange for a variety of payback schemes); this was the Trump model, previously discussed.

In a blatant violation of NIGC regulations, one of the slot machine companies agreed to co-sign the loan in exchange for the verbal agreement that they would be the only company with slot machines at the new casino. Had such a violation been committed to paper, the National Indian Gaming Commission would have nullified it, so it was shrewdly kept as a verbal unwritten agreement.

As a slot machine vendor and not casino operators, the original funding group did not budget for basic casino supplies, payroll for staff during training, or even enough to do some of the finishing work on the structure. There was no money budgeted for signage. They did not even have money for staff uniforms or food and beverage supplies for the restaurant and bar. Even more troubling, there was no money to pave the mud-hole parking lot in this challenging terrain.

To further complicate issues, the architect chosen by the business committee designed the casino with, frankly, some absolute absurdities (and financial nightmares) in the plans. Although lights and light poles had been designed for the muddy parking lot, there were no plans to run electricity to the lights. The roof was not designed to handle the weight of the HVAC (heating, ventilation, air conditioning) system necessary for the property and when that flaw was discovered, apparently the designers decided "what-the-heck" and added an unplanned second floor to the casino to have a place to put the unit. (And of course, each time it came on it shook the entire building, like a small earthquake on the second floor.)

A server room, housing for multiple heat-generating computer servers for the Class II bingo machines, had neither ventilation nor air conditioning. (Measured heat levels in the room eventually reached more than 115°.) No study had been made of the water supply system and the well that fed it. When the water was turned on, large chunks of minerals (some over two inches in diameter) rushed through pipes and instantly destroyed portions of internal plumbing of the building. A huge lobby centerpiece fireplace faced the cashier cage so that if any long lines developed there, the customers would be rotisserized by the flames.

The cashier cage itself was strategically positioned as near as possible to the front door, making it easy for customers to cash-out and not have to be "bothered" by walking by slot machines to spend their winnings; as if it was designed to keep money from going back into slot machines. At the same time this location of the cashier cage also made it convenient for any would-be thieves to easily exit the casino without hindrance. And, with no "panic button" or alarms in the cage plans (and being only a few miles from the Canadian border), the cage location was really an asset to any potential robber(s).

A floor-to-ceiling "two-way-mirror" in the General Manager's office looking onto the casino floor had the serious problem that if the lights were on in the office, then the occupants could not see the casino floor but all the customers on the floor could observe whatever might be going on in the office. On the casino floor, in-floor wiring conduit was set in concrete rather than in a duct system, so once slot machines were placed on the floor the only way they could be moved was to cut through concrete and redirect wiring. Enough kitchen equipment had been ordered to outfit a large university cafeteria (vast overkill); but no dishwashing equipment had been ordered; nor ice machines or pumping stations for the bar. Additionally, there was no storage space for food and supplies in this remote area where all deliveries halt during the several road-impassible months.

A number of planning-related violations of the NIGC Minimum Internal Control Standards included: No way to securely lock away bingo paper (which has a cash equivalent value); a cashiers' vault that could be entered through an unprotected drop-ceiling; the "vault" was constructed with solid kitchen cabinets, allowing for no view of assets (by surveillance cameras) when the doors were closed; no controlled access to gaming servers; no controlled access to surveillance equipment (which itself was below minimum requirements for the projected income of the casino, and had been selected, provided, and installed by the business committee-owned cable television company without competitive bid; and a host of other federal violations.

The planning did not take into account the high winds common in the town and within a few weeks of opening, large metal sheets of roofing were flapping freely and flying around the parking lot like frisbees thrown toward windshields. (Yes there were insurance claims by several car owners.) Within a month the winds had also destroyed the large freestanding outdoor sign.

On top of these construction-related nightmares, the project was equally plagued with organizational problems. There had been no planning for a players' club, for a location for employees to take meals, for lockers for employees to store purses and coats, nor for almost any of the back-of-the-house operations (like slot technicians, casino audit, alcohol storage, a surveillance room, etc.), as well as many more lack-of-experience omissions.

As if this shopping list of troubles were not enough, the HR (human resources) department, like finance, was kept separate from the casino and controlled exclusively by the business committee. HR positioned itself more as employee advocates than an entity to protect the casino. Consequently, there were no job testing policies (other than in-house conducted drug testing by a convicted drug felon who recently had been released from prison), and people were offered jobs literally based on judgments like, "You look like a cashier."

Among that kind of HR-mandated gems were the cashiers and supervisors from the Tribe's previous small bingo casino. At that property, one cashier had accepted a $5 bill from a customer and given the customer change of two twenties and a ten. The excuse was that the five-dollar bill had been mistaken for a fifty-dollar bill because a zero had been drawn beside the five. I reviewed the case file and looked at the bill in question: the zero was drawn with a black "Sharpie" marker; I still have photographs of that five-dollar bill. Sadly, these employees *really and truly* were *that* oblivious to their jobs; they *really* did not notice.

It was with this backdrop that I positioned the grand opening as the biggest event to hit Montana since Little Big Horn. After talking with the business committee and its hired president, I began positioning this crapulent, remote, and icy perdition as the Las Vegas of the Northwest. It was my plan to bring the wealthy white tourist from Glacier National Park to the casino and avoid catering to the local population. I genuinely believed that building a glitter-place casino for no reason other than taking money from the already downtrodden local population would be both a viciously genocidal aggression and a financial disaster. How could we possibly justify creating a casino to cater only to people whose annual income was less than $9,000?

The real disturbing thing about these atrocious descriptions is that they are not isolated. They are not particularly unique to that Tribe nor its business committee (except, of course, the death of the Elvis); nor are they an indictment of any particular practices. Rather, such anecdotes of dysfunctional episodes are symptomatic of the all-to-frequent landscape of Indian gaming in remote, isolated areas and of inexperienced, nearly sequestered, Tribes.

While the NIGC offers some helpful guidelines for such Tribes, it is more common that groups like NIGA (the National Indian Gaming

Association), the trade association of gaming Tribes, offer regulator training and a host of other assisting services. That double-edged sword of regulation has kept some Tribes from being able to make their own decisions to reach out to experts who do not fall within the one-size-fits-all requirements of IGRA.

For this Montana project, I brought in the recently fired Oklahoma regulator/ex-cop, David Cook, to bring some semblance of organization and operational order to the new casino. David, himself being Native (Choctaw), entered the project with some degree of affinity to the day-to-day realities of life on a remote reservation; the very realities that had given rise to the majority of the issues I had encountered.

David immediately set upon the tasks of smoothing out the operation and installing Minimum Internal Control Standards (that I had written the previous year for the Ottawa Tribe in the mid-West, when I helped developed their casino). He effectively created a viable operation and he had plenty of time to do so; he had recently become unemployed in Oklahoma.

Cook's Oklahoma unemployment had come about after the implosion of those broad-based reforms that we had instituted for that treasurer's Oklahoma Tribe. The Tribal government was ousted and the casino was seized by the treasurer's most vehement foes, who almost immediately reinstated many of the employees that David and I had fired as we uncovered the various rip-offs.

Among the grievances against the ousted Tribal Council was the charge that they had hired a Las Vegas gangster to steal parts of Las Vegas and hide it on Indian land. According to the charges against the council, I had stolen the iconic "Fabulous Las Vegas" sign from the strip, transported it to Oklahoma, and buried it on Tribal land.

Apparently gestated by a particularly playful television commercial in which I "stole" the spirit of Las Vegas and brought it to this casino, the implication of the charges against the Council was that under their direction millions of dollars of cash flow had ended (presumably from some of the illegal activities Cook and I uncovered). The supposedly lost millions (that used to go to the tribal members who worked at the casino) now supposedly had been diverted to various Tribal funds. No, seriously, these were among the allegations against the Tribe's

Governor, the Secretary, and the Treasurer who had instigated the reforms in the first place.

Introducing me to the Oklahoma project in the first place, the treasurer had introduced me to Tribal Governor Ken Blanchard. I soon learned that Ken kept a notebook filled with photographs of the homes and living conditions of his people casino gaming. The stark images of poverty from the Appalachia of my own childhood were practically images of luxury compared to the bleakly severe deficiencies and abject poverty suffered by Ken's people. Page after page of Blanchard's scrapbook served to remind him and show me the necessity of economic development programs, health care, housing, and jobs provided by casino gaming on his Tribal land.

Not only was my mission clear, from talks with Ken Blanchard, but his vision was clear as well. Ken Blanchard had a mission in life and that casino was part of that mission. Talks with him were among those few-in-a-lifetime defining moments and my decision to work in Oklahoma rather than run back to Trump was driven by Blanchard's sincerity, his vision, and the mission he had given me.

A little more than a year later, after a long and expensive battle, when the voters of Oklahoma finally empowered their governor to sign a gaming compact with Tribes, Governor Blanchard was with Oklahoma Governor Brad Henry at one minute after midnight on January First when the law went into effect. The two Governors signed the history-making document and Blanchard became the first Tribal leader to sign a compact with the State of Oklahoma.

After a very few months, for the first time in its 13-year history, the casino was a money-making operation for the Tribe. As reported in *Indian Gaming Business Magazine*, the Tribe's revenue increased by $30 million. The majority of the exploitive "electronic bingo device" machine vendors were out and the first Class II games produced by giant IGT were shipping to the casino; and for the first time in the Oklahoma casino industry, professionals from the industry were providing their expertise to Tribal government.

It was this kind of visionary leadership that should have made Kenneth Blanchard a legend among his people and for generations have his name spoken with the same reverence as the first great Shawnee leader, Tecumseh. But, alas, such was not to be the fate of

Blanchard's selfless dedication to his Tribe and to his people. And such was not to be the legacy of either the Compact with Oklahoma nor the casino.

Unfortunately for the Tribal membership, the supporters of all of those fired employees and kicked-out vendors spent the next two years marshaling their political forces to oust Blanchard, Treasurer Russell Ellis, and the other Tribal crusaders for a legal and profitable casino. After a bitterly fought election and absurd charges and countercharges, the Blanchard team was defeated in the election.

As a backlash to it all, the Tribal opposition leader had me followed, had me shot at, and paid a hacker to attempt to copy the hard drive of my computer. In a series of bad-action movie scenes of high-speed chases, hidden recording devices, and wanna-be thugs, the new government was determined to intimidate me into turning against Blanchard. I, personally, was targeted in the campaign against him with death threats, being followed to and from the casino, and a series of posters claiming that I never worked for Trump and that he had obtained a court-order to have me stop making that claim. Another flier claimed that I was an operative of an organized crime "family" that had decided to use Oklahoma as a stepping stone to syphon enough cash to buy Las Vegas, all of Las Vegas.

Around the same time, an FBI agent approached me and forewarned that the Justice Department had been monitoring one Blanchard's chief opponent for years in drug sales and fund embezzlement investigations. "You can't let this guy win the election," the agent warned me during the campaign. But it was too late; despite my best efforts to help Blanchard, including writing him a campaign plan, he was out. Shortly thereafter, so were David Cook and 135 others, including myself.

The Montana stories and the Oklahoma stories are indicative only of the paradoxes and complexities of Indian country; enigmas born from the relationship our government has had with Native Americans and of the multifarious history of Indian Gaming. While the Indian Gaming world is filled with perfectly functional and in fact, stellar models for casino operations, there is no escaping the complications gestated by the history of the relationships.

Undeniably, I have spent a lot of years in Indian country; first as that displaced 1960s radical following the Wounded Knee struggles for sovereignty, and later as a developer, operator, and financier of casinos on behalf of various Tribes across the country. I have been either fortunate or cursed, depending on one's perspective, to have avocation and skills in both arenas.

At this point, it is probably germane to tell you that I am a white Southerner with a fixation on 1950s westerns as the great passion plays of my culture; and I grew up thinking the unrelated Jackson boys (Andrew and Stonewall) were the good guys. So I suspect my original journeys to Native America were probably less about historical reparation and more about the romanticism of reliving Sam Houston's being adopted into the Cherokee Nation, Davy Crockett's fight against Andrew Jackson's notorious Indian Removal Act, or some other fanciful (if not paternally racist) imagined adventures of my gambler hero Doc Holliday's time living with the Ute people.

While distributing the radical Native American newspaper, Akwesasne Notes, playing guitar and singing *Custer Died for Your Sins* on stage with my friend Kanghi Duta (Floyd Westerman), or raising money, support, and "supplies" for Wounded Knee, the romanticism melded with the zeitgeist of the early 1970s political radicalism. Organizing and demonstrating with AIM leadership and TAIMSG; secret meetings with Tuscarora leaders; and a whirlwind of rallies, gatherings, and protests; all facilitated that transition a decade and a half before IGRA.

Still, I really do not know how even to begin describing the transition I observed in Native American life in the 20th and 21st centuries. Consider the Middle-America ethos of "work hard and get out of poverty," against something more akin to being jerked from the lowest depths of degradation to seemingly overnight controlling and self-regulating hundreds of millions of dollars in cash flow.

The fact remains that like Hollywood's insultingly fictionalized "Comancharos," modern-day non-Indians offering financing, slot machine deals, management consulting, and other "services" are fundamentally not unlike those heinous exploiters of the past. Reaping a 400% profit that would be criminal usury in many states but is routine at Indian casinos, is simply the modern-day equivalent of trading beads and trinkets for Manhattan Island.

I would be seriously remiss if I did not make it perfectly clear that the myth of rich Indians rolling in the wealth from gambling empires is in fact just that: a myth. Yes, there are extremely profitable Indian casinos and some wealthy Tribal members who have reap the benefits of those profits; that is true. But the number of tribes that fit that category are countable on one hand. Of the just-under-500 Indian casinos, those tales of opulence are limited to less than 2%. The majority of the multi-billion-dollar revenue goes to social programs, educational programs, clothing, housing, and basic sustenance for tribal members; and even with then tens of thousands of Indians are still struggling on the lowest rungs of the American financial ladder. Still, they are improving and getting there.

For me, at least, the proverbial silver lining to all of this is exactly what Max Osceola said following the purchase of the Hard Rock chain: *Our ancestors sold Manhattan for trinkets. We're going to buy Manhattan back, one burger at a time.*

It was Osceola's revenge.

Glossary of Casino Terms Only Insiders Know

25 CFR: Title 25 of the United States Code, dealing with Indians, as defined in the Code of Federal Regulations and published in the Federal Register

542: The section of 25 CFR that lists the minimum internal control standards for an Indian casino

86: To remove someone from the casino, throw them out

Action: Amount of all wagers made either by an individual, at a specific game, or for the entire casino

AIM: American Indian Movement. Radical Indian advocacy movement formed in 1968 to address sovereignty, treaties, spirituality, and leadership. The primary group identified as "occupying" Wounded Knee South Dakota during the 1973 siege. The author was a co-founder of AIMSG (American Indian Movement Support Group) that same year

Badge: A casino employee's identification/license, which must be worn at all times when at work

Bank: The generic name for the money used to replenish cashiers, tables, etc.

BIA: Bureau of Indian Affairs, U.S. Department of Interior

Big Bertha: An oversized slot machine put on the casino floor as a marketing device to attract players

Black Book: List of people "86'd" from the casino (the term comes from the Nevada Gaming Control Board's notorious "black book of excluded persons" prohibited from entering a casino

Boss: Any of the management team of a casino

Break out: The first casino where someone works; the first job at a casino

Butterworth: Landmark 1981 court case before the United States Court of Appeals for the Fifth Circuit which allowed the Seminole Tribe of Florida to operate high stakes bingo in Florida. The precedent-setting case helped open the door to Indian Gaming nationwide

BV: Bill validator. The electronic device in a slot machine that accepts cash or credit tickets

Cabazon: 1987 US Supreme Court case California v. Cabazon Band of Mission Indians, 480 U.S. 202 which overturned laws prohibiting gambling on US Indian reservations

Cage: Area where cashiers are located; where players "cash out" and collect their winnings

Card: The magnetic-striped player card issued to players to insert into a slot machine to track play

Carpet Joint: An upscale casino (so named because of carpet on the floors)

Cash Equivalents: Documents, financial instruments other than cash, or anything else of representative value to which the gaming operation has assigned a monetary value. A cash equivalent includes, but is not limited to, tokens, chips, coupons, vouchers, payout slips and tickets, and other items to which a gaming operation has assigned an exchange value

Central Credit: A privately owned casino player credit bureau since 1956, making decades of gaming credit history and gaming transaction data on millions of casino patrons available to casino operators for consideration when extending casino credit

Check or Check: Insider term for a chip used at table games

Chicks: The Chickasaw Tribe of Oklahoma, owners of the largest casino in the world (WinStar World) and more than a dozen other casinos

Class II: A designation created by the Indian Gaming Regulatory Act (IGRA) defining bingo, electronic bingo, pull tabs, and non-house-banked card games

Class III: A designation created by the Indian Gaming Regulatory Act (IGRA) defining all casino games that are not designated "Class II"

Club: The players club of a casino with membership defined by use of a player tracking card to identify a patron's activity to the casino

Coin-in: The amount of play a slot machine receives (not taking into account the payouts); cash played plus TITO (see definition below) tickets played, plus earned (or won) credits played.

Commission: A gaming control authority, either Tribal, Federal, or State

Commissioners: Elected or appointed members of a gaming control authority

Comp: Complimentary or free

Compact: A contract between Tribal governments and a State government

Compliance: A casino department responsible for adhering to TICS and MICS

Count: A special team of employees (with special pocketless uniforms) in a special room under tight security, for counting coins and currency

Count Machine: A high speed electromechanical machine used to count cash or coins

Count Room: Secured room where the count is performed in which the cash and cash equivalents are counted

Credits: Betting units based on the denomination of the machine. For example a quarter machine (25) with $20 put into the machine, there would be 80 credits available for play

Denom: Denomination of credits:

Drop: The total amount of money, tickets, and coupons removed from any slot, table or kiosk the amount of money taken in by the casino for bets

Drop box: A locked box either inside a slot machine or at a table game where player wagers are stored. Access to the key(s) to open a drop box are usually under the strict control of the TGA

Drop Team: The team of employees who participate in the removal of drop boxes from machines and tables and transportation of the drop to the count room. Sometimes the drop team also does the count; sometimes the count team is separate

EPROM: Acronym for erasable programmable read-only memory. In slot machines, these are the chips that house the math of the game

Federal Register: is the official daily publication of the federal government of the United States listing government agency rules, proposed rules, and public notices

Fee Land: Land purchased by a Tribe outside the boundaries of Trust Land and not subject to legal restrictions against alienation or encumbrance, and not eligible for gaming

Fill: a transaction in which a supply of chips, tokens, or coins are replaced during game play

Flag: The brand-name of a hotel chain (Hilton, Marriott, etc.) attached to a casino hotel as part of a franchise or operational deal

Floor: Supervisor in table games (also sometimes called a "pit boss")

Frequency: A measure of slot machine performance; a machine with high frequency has a greater chance of consistently hitting smaller payouts; high frequency goes arm in arm with low volatility. Low frequency machines mean that payouts are rare; such machines are usually highly volatile

Grind Joint: A casino that "grinds" money from a patron in the lowest denominations (one penny at a time). Grind joints are "low-class" cheap casinos

Hand Pay: Either a mechanical or regulatory situation in which a slot machine cannot pay the patron in the typical manner, requiring the casino staff to pay the customer out manually. This is most common with any payout greater than $1,199.99 ($1,200 triggers the federal requirement for a W2-G form)

Hard Count: Process for counting coins in a casino

Hold: The gross profit of a slot machine or table: amount wagered minus player winnings (payouts)

Hopper: For slot machines that still use coins (rather than paper money or TITO tickets) this is the place where coins are held in the machine

House Banked: Games played against the casino; the win (player loss) goes to the casino rather than to other players (in a non-house banked game, the profit from the game goes to the player rather than to the casino)

IGRA: The 1988 Indian Gaming Regulatory Act; Public L 100–497, 25 United States Code § 2701 et seq

Indian Country: Native American jargon for the general community of Native American Indians, inside or outside of sovereignty

Indian Time: Also called IST (Indian Standard Time). In many Native American cultures, the concept that things will happen when they are supposed to and no sooner. This is often a headache for non-Indian casino operators or developers who have a more anal approach to appointment times

Joint: Casino-speak for a casino

Keys: Rooms. The number of rooms in a hotel is referred to as the number of keys

Kobetron: A proprietary device (licensed by a Florida-based technology company of the same name) used to authenticate and measure the accuracy of a slot machine EPROM chip. The chip has a Kobetron signature algorithm which is typically verified by a TGA before a slot machine is placed on a casino floor

License: A gaming commission issued permit to work in or do business with a casino; issued following a background investigation

Man Trap: Used as the entrance to the count room or the cage, a man trap is a small room with an entry door on one wall and an exit door on the opposite wall. One door of a mantrap cannot be unlocked and opened until the opposite door has been closed and locked

Marker: A short-term loan or credit line provided by the casino to qualified players; typically secured by a counter check.

Match Play: A popular casino promotion in which "free play" (at either a slot machine or table game) is awarded to the patron provided that the patron gambles an equal amount of their own money

Meters: Either electromechanical or virtual counting devices inside a slot machine. Meters record a variety of slot machine functions (credits in, credits out, payouts, actual cash, tickets, etc.).

MICS: Minimum Internal Control Standards; rules to assure integrity of casino, assets, cash, and the casino games

Multi-denom: Slot machines that are capable of assigning varying denominations to credits (penny, nickel, dime, quarter, fifty cents, dollar, five dollar, $100, etc.)

Native: Relating to the indigenous peoples of the Americas; relating to Indians. While there is an entire polemic about whether to refer to Native Peoples as Natives, Indian, or by Tribal-language names, Tribal casinos are generally referred to by the Tribes as "Indian Casinos"

NIGA: National Indian Gaming Association. Not to be confused with the NIGC (as it often is), this is the trade association of Tribal Casinos and includes an "associate member" status for vendors to the industry.

NIGC: National Indian Gaming Commission. Established by IGRA to regulate Indian gaming to promote Tribal economic development and maintain the integrity of the Indian gaming industry, and to ensure that tribes are the primary beneficiaries of Indian gaming activities.

Opinion Letter: A letter (written by either the NIGC or an attorney) presented to a gaming authority arguing whether a particular game is legal or not legal for play under the provisions of the Indian Gaming Regulatory Act or 25 C.F.R

Par: The payout percentages of a slot machines; opposite of hold

Par Sheet: A proprietary document provided by slot machine manufacturers showing how particular slot machine is designed, including the pay table, reel strips, and any other pertinent information to rules of the game and payouts

Pencil Power: The ability of a casino executive to grant comps to a player regardless of the formula provided by the player tracking system

Progressive: Slot machine, with a payoff indicator, in which the jackpot increases as the game is played (a deferred payout). The jackpot amount is accumulated, displayed on a machine, and will remain until a player lines up the jackpot symbols that result in the progressive amount being paid

Pull Tabs: A gambling card with a paper tab that can be pulled back to reveal a row of symbols or numbers with cash or prizes for matching symbols. These can also be electronic facsimiles of the cards. IGRA classifies Pull Tabs as Class II gaming devices.

Rake: The method for the casino to receive compensation for hosting poker or other card games; the casino takes a set percentage of each pot or a flat fee for each bet made (rather than taking the winnings as in a "house-banked" game)

Rev Share: Revenue share: the most common rental method for Indian casinos to lease slot machines from a manufacturer. A rev share lease is based on win-per-unit and is usually 80% for the Tribe and 20% for the vendor

Rez: Indian country speak for "reservation"

RFB: Room-Food-and-Beverage. The highest "comp" level at a casino, indicating the player is a big gambler and has earned (from their play) everything free

Sawdust Joint: A cheap or low-class casino. The term comes from the original Las Vegas casinos that had sawdust floors rather than carpet on their floors

Shill: A casino employee whose job assignment is to pretend to be a player, using casino money, to create an atmosphere of excitement and give the illusion that a particular game or games are popular and being played

Soft Count: The process for counting paper money; soft count rooms are the most secure places in the casino due to the large amounts of cash that can be on hand at any one time

Status: A player's ranking within a casino's players club; usually silver, gold, or platinum. The ranking indicates (among other things) a minimum amount of (casino) win (player loss) the player has in a calendar year

Steppers: An electromechanical reel slot machine, as opposed to the more common video-reel slot machines. These machines physically resemble old spinning-reel mechanical slot machines

Surveillance: This is a physical location rather than an activity. This is the location in the "back of the house" at a casino where the surveillance of digital video recorders, camera control, and observational staff are located

System: The computer system for casino accounting, player tracking, and interoperability between slot machines

Tables: All casino games that are not slot machines. Table games: blackjack, craps, poker, roulette, etc.

TGA: Tribal Gaming Authority (also often called Tribal Gaming Commission); the Tribally appointed regulatory body for a particular Tribe's gaming operations

The Act: IGRA: the 1988 Indian Gaming Regulatory Act; Public L 100–497, 25 United States Code § 2701 et seq

TICS: Tribal Internal Control Standards. These are the rules a Tribe adopts for its gaming control authority to assure integrity of Tribal assets, cash, and the casino games

Tier A: Indian casino with annual gross gaming revenues of more than $3 million but not more than $8 million

Tier B: Indian casino with annual gross gaming revenues of more than $8 million but not more than $15 million

Tier C: Indian casino with annual gross gaming revenues of more than $15 million

Title 31: The anti-money laundering act of the U.S. Code. Title 31 certification is required for all cage employees

56

Gary Green

TITO: "Ticket In / Ticket Out" technology which prints out a bar-coded piece of paper at a slot machine, which can then either be redeemed for cash, or inserted for play into other TITO machines. Originally developed by International Game Technology (IGT) and Casino Data Systems (CDS) but now used by all slot machines (with a royalty paid to the two originating companies)

Toke: Tip, gratuity

Trust: Land held in trust by the United States government on behalf of a Native American Tribe; the federal government holds legal title but the beneficial interest allegedly remains with the tribe

Vault: This is the physical location behind the cage, where the bank is stored

Vendor: Casino-speak for a slot machine manufacturer

Volatility: A measure of how closely a slot machine will perform to its theoretical hold percentage over time (over millions of combinations the actual hold percentage of a volatile slot machine program may at any point in time vary considerably from its theoretical hold percentage. A machine with low volatility has a greater chance of hitting smaller payouts along the way with less of a chance of hitting the larger jackpots. High volatility machines mean a player can win large amounts, but can also lose very quickly as well

W2G: IRS form W-2G to report gambling winnings and any federal income tax withheld on those winnings

WAP: Wide Area Progressive. A progressive slot machine that is linked to other slot machines in other casinos and play on those machines affect a progressively increasing payout amount. As wagers are placed, the progressive meters on all of the linked machines increase

Win: For casino insider this is just the opposite of what it means for players. This is how much money the casino makes from players; this is player's losses —which mean casino's win

WPU: Win per unit. The amount of money a slot machine makes (coin-in minus payouts to players); also the average win of all slot machines on a casino floor

WPUPD: Win per unit per day

APPENDIX

Following is the text of the Trump management contract with the Twenty-Nine Palms Band of Mission Indians. This contract, like all NIGC-approved management contracts, is public record and requires neither permission of the tribe or the company to review. It is presented here in its entirety to show a template for hundreds of such agreements, and it is presented because of the historical significance of an Indian casino contract entered into by the man who became President of the United States. That, alone, is probably one of history's most significant landmarks of Indian relations with the United States. Please note that there are large blank sections and incomplete sentences throughout the contract; these have been redacted by the National Indian Gaming Commission and kept from public view. Section 20 of the agreement shows President Trump's signature page for the agreement.

GAMING FACILITY
MANAGEMENT AGREEMENT

THIS AMENDED AND RESTATED GAMING FACILITY MANAGEMENT AGREEMENT (this "Agreement") is made as of the day of March 2002, by and between the **TWENTY-NINE PALMS BAND OF LUISENO MISSION INDIANS OF CALIFORNIA,** a sovereign Native American nation, with offices at 46-200 Harrison Place, Coachella, California 92236 (the "Tribe"), the **TWENTY-NINE PALMS ENTERPRISES CORPORATION,** a Federal corporation chartered by the Tribe pursuant to 25 U.S.C. Section 477, with offices at 46-200 Harrison Place, Coachella, California 92236 ("the Enterprise") and **THCR MANAGEMENT SERVICES, LLC,** a Delaware limited liability company with offices at 1000 Boardwalk, Atlantic City, New Jersey 08401.

RECITALS:

The Tribe is a federally recognized Indian Tribe, which possesses sovereign governmental powers pursuant to the Tribe's recognized powers of self-government. The Tribe occupies certain property located in Coachella, Riverside County, California, more specifically described on Exhibit A attached hereto, as "Indian lands" pursuant to 25 U.S.C. 2703(4) (the "Property"). The Tribe currently operates a Class II gaming facility on the Property.

The Tribe desires to further develop the Property to promote increased tribal economic development, self-sufficiency and strong tribal government.

In order to obtain the benefit of Manager's management, marketing and technical experience and expertise, the Tribe and Manager entered into a Gaming Facility Management Agreement dated as of April 27, 2000.

The Tribe chartered the Enterprise to conduct Class II and Class III Gaming pursuant to the Indian Gaming Regulatory Act and the Compact at the Facility, and transferred all of its right, title and interest in and to the Facility to the Enterprise pursuant to an Assignment and Bill of Sale dated July 5, 2001.

With the assistance of Trump Hotels & Casino Resorts Development Company, LLC, the Enterprise intends to design, finance, construct, furnish and equip a permanent Class III gaming resort on the Property, which shall include a new casino facility, a hotel and other amenities and the renovation of the Tribe's existing Class II gaming facility.

The Tribe, the Enterprise and Manager desire to amend and restate in its entirety the April 27, 2000 Gaming Facility Management Agreement in order to conform such agreement to comments received from the NIGC.

This Agreement is entered into pursuant to the Indian Gaming Regulatory Act of 1988, PL 100-497, 25 U.S.C. 2701 et seq. (the "IGRA") as that statute may be amended. All gaming conducted at the Facility will at all times comply with the IGRA, applicable Tribal law and the Compact.

SECTION 1
AMENDED AND RESTATED AGREEMENT; DEFINITIONS

<u>Amended and Restated Agreement.</u> **This Agreement amends and restates in its entirety the Gaming Facility Management** Agreement entered into by the Tribe and Manager as of April 27, 2000.

<u>Definitions.</u> As they are used in this Agreement, the terms listed below shall have the meaning assigned to them in this Section:

"Affiliate" means as to Manager, the Enterprise or the Tribe, any corporation, partnership, limited liability company, joint venture, trust, department or agency or individual controlled by or controlling, directly or indirectly, Manager, the Enterprise or the Tribe.

"Articles of Association" shall mean the Articles of Association of The Twenty-Nine Palms Band of Luiseno Mission Indians of California as adopted by the Tribe on March 1, 1972 and approved by the Secretary of the Interior.

"BIA" shall mean the Bureau of Indian Affairs of the Department of the Interior of the United States of America.

"Capital Budget" shall mean the capital budget described in Section 3.10.

"Capital Replacement(s)" shall mean any alteration or rebuilding or renovation of the Facility, and any replacement of Furnishings and Equipment, the cost of which is capitalized and depreciated, rather than being expensed, applying generally accepted accounting principles, as described in Section 3.10.

"Capital Replacement Reserve" shall mean the reserve described in Section 3.12, into which periodic contributions are paid pursuant to Section 3.13.

"Charter" shall mean the Federal Charter of Incorporation of the Enterprise approved by the U.S. Department of the Interior on February 16, 2001 and ratified by the Tribe on March 28, 2001 pursuant to 25 U.S.C. Section 477.

"Class II Gaming" shall mean Class II Gaming as defined in the IGRA. "Class III Gaming" shall mean Class III Gaming as defined in the IGRA.

"Commencement Date" shall mean the first date that the approximately 50,000 square foot planned casino addition to the Facility is complete and open to the public for Gaming, which shall be the date upon which management services begin under this Agreement.

"Compact" shall mean the Tribal-State Compact between the Tribe and the State of California regarding Class III Gaming, executed by the Tribe on October 1, 1999 and signed by the Secretary of the Interior on May 5, 2000 and published in the Federal Register as provided in 25 U.S.C. 2710(d)(8)(D) on May 16, 2000; as the same may, from time to time, be amended, or such other Compact that may be substituted therefor.

"Compensation" shall mean the direct salaries and wages paid to, or accrued for the benefit of, any employee, including incentive compensation, together with all fringe benefits payable to or accrued for the benefit of such executive or other employee, including employer's contribution under FICA, unemployment compensation or other employment taxes, pension fund contributions, workers' compensation, group life, accident and health insurance premiums and costs, and profit sharing, severance, retirement, disability, relocation, housing and other similar benefits.

"Confidential Information" shall mean the information described in Section 8.22.

"Depository Account" shall mean the bank account described in Section 3.17.2.

"Disbursement Account" shall mean the bank account described in Section 3.17.3.

"Early Termination Fee" shall mean^{r-}

"Effective Date" shall mean the date five (5) days following the date on which all of the following listed conditions are satisfied: written approval of this Agreement is granted by the Chairman of the NIGC; written approval of a Tribal Gaming Code is granted by the Chairman of the NIGC; written confirmation that the Tribe and the State (to the extent required by the Compact) have approved background investigations of Manager; Manager has received a certified copy of the Tribal Resolutions adopted by the Tribe in accordance with the Tribe's governing documents and the Corporate Resolutions adopted by the Enterprise in accordance with the Charter authorizing the execution of this Agreement; execution of the Compact by the Secretary of the Interior and publication in the Federal Register as provided in 25 U.S.C. 2710(d)(8)(D); receipt by Manager of all applicable licenses for or related to management of the Facility; and Manager has satisfied itself that the Tribal Gaming Code and any other code adopted by the Tribe relative to any of the documents referenced in this Agreement do not have a material adverse effect on Manager's ability to operate the Facility under this Agreement.

"Emergency Condition" shall have the meaning set forth in Section 3.11.

"Enterprise" shall mean the "Twenty-Nine Palms Enterprises Corporation" chartered under 25 U.S.C. 477 by the Tribe to engage in Class II and Class III Gaming at the Facility and any other lawful commercial activity allowed in the Facility including, but not limited to the sale of alcohol, tobacco, gifts and souvenirs; or any ancillary non-Gaming activity within the Facility generally related to Class II or Class III Gaming.

"Enterprise Bank Accounts" shall mean those accounts described in Section

"Enterprise Employee" shall mean all Employees who are assigned to work at

"Enterprise Employee Policies" shall mean those employee policies described in Section 3.6.2.

"Excess Funds" shall have the meaning described in Section 5.4.1 so long as the Transfer and Deposit Agreement may be in effect, and thereafter "Excess Funds" shall have the meaning described in Section 5.4.2.

"Facility" shall mean all buildings, structures and improvements located on the Property used in connection with gaming or used for the operation of the Enterprise, and all fixtures, Furnishings and Equipment attached to, forming a part of, or necessary for the operation of such buildings, structures and improvements.

"Financing Agreements" shall mean all loan agreements, indentures, notes, security agreements and other documents to be entered into between the Tribe and/or the Enterprise and one or more Lenders pursuant to which the financing is issued including, without limitation, the Loan Agreement.

"Fiscal Year" shall mean the period commencing on January 1 of each year and ending on December 31 of such year, except that for purposes of calculating the Management Fee, the first Fiscal Year shall be deemed to commence upon the Commencement Date and end on December 31 of such year.

"Furnishings and Equipment" shall mean all furniture, furnishings and equipment required for the operation of the Facility, including, without limitation: cashier, money sorting and money counting equipment, surveillance and communication equipment and security equipment; electronic lottery terminals, video games of chance, table games, bingo blowers and equipment, electronic displays, Class II pull-tab dispensers, table games, pari-mutuel betting equipment and other Class II and Class III gaming equipment permitted pursuant to the Compact and the IGRA; office furnishings and equipment; specialized equipment necessary for the operation of any portion of the Facility for accessory purposes, including equipment for entertainment facilities, hospitality facilities, kitchens, laundries, dry cleaning, cocktail lounges, restaurants, public rooms, commercial and parking spaces and recreational facilities; all decor, special effects and artwork; and all other furnishings and equipment hereafter located and installed in or about the Facility which are used in the operation of the Facility in accordance with the standards set forth in this Agreement.

"Gaming" shall mean any and all activities defined as Class II and Class III Gaming.

"General Manager" shall mean the person supplied by Manager and employed by the Enterprise to direct the operation of the Facility.

"Generally Accepted Accounting Principles or GAAP" shall mean those principles defined by the Financial Accounting Standards Board.

"Gross Gaming Revenue (Win)" shall mean the net win from gaming activities which is the difference between gaming wins and losses before deducting costs and expenses.

"Gross Revenues" shall mean all revenues of any nature derived directly or indirectly from the Facility including, without limitation, Gross Gaming Revenue (Win), food and beverage sales, and other rental or other receipts from lessees, sublessees, licensees and concessionaires (but not the gross receipts of such lessees, sublessees, licensees or concessionaires, provided that such lessees, sublessees, and licensees and concessionaires are not subsidiaries or affiliates of Manager), and revenue recorded for Promotional Allowances, but excluding any taxes the Tribe is allowed to assess pursuant to Section 7.

"House Bank" shall mean the amount of cash, chips, tokens and plaques that Manager from time to time determines necessary to have at the Facility daily to meet its cash needs.

"IGRA" shall mean the Indian Gaming Regulatory Act of 1988, PL 100-497, 25 U.S.C. 2701 *et seq.*, same may, from time to time, be amended.

"Internal Control Systems" shall mean the systems described in Section 3.16.

"Legal Requirements" shall mean any and all present and future judicial, administrative, and tribal rulings or decisions, and any and all present and future federal, state, local, and tribal laws, codes, rules, regulations, permits, licenses and certificates, in any way applicable to the Tribe, Manager, the Property, the Facility, and the Enterprise, including without limitation, the IGRA, the Compact, and the Tribal Gaming Code.

"Lender" shall mean First National Bank, as Administrative Agent, together with the "Lenders" identified in the Financing Agreement(s).

"Loan Agreement" shall mean the Loan Agreement dated October 17, 2001, by and among The Twenty-Nine Palms Enterprises Corporation, The Twenty-Nine Palms Band of Luiseno Mission Indians of California, the Lenders referred to therein, and First National Bank, together with all documents that constitute "Loan Documents" as defined therein.

"Management Agreement" shall mean this Agreement and may be referred **to herein** as the "Agreement."

"Management Fee" shall mean the management fee described in Section 5.1.

"Manager" shall mean TI-ICR Management Services, LLC, its successors and assigns.

"Manager Advance" shall mean any funds advanced by Manager or its Affiliates to the Enterprise, including on account of the Minimum Guaranteed Monthly Payment or the Manager Guaranty.

"Manager Guaranty" shall mean

"Manager Proprietary Information" shall mean the information described in Section 8.22.

"Material Breach" shall mean such material breach as described in Section 10.3.

"Member of The Tribal Government" shall have the meaning described in Section 9.5.

"Minimum Balance" shall mean the amount described in Section 3.17.1.

"Minimum Guaranteed Monthly Payment" shall mean that payment due the Tribe each month commencing in the month after the Commencement Date occurs in accordance with 25 U.S.C. 2711(b)(3) and Section 5.5 hereof.

"National Indian Gaming Commission" or **"NIGC"** shall mean the commission established pursuant to 25 U.S.C. 2704.

"Net Revenues" shall mean the sum of "Net Revenues (Gaming)" and **"Net Revenues (Other)."**

"Net Revenues (Gaming)" shall mean Gross Gaming Revenue (Win), of the Enterprise from Class H or Class III gaming less all gaming related Operating Expenses, excluding the Management Fee, and less the retail value of any Promotional Allowances, and less the following revenues actually received by the Enterprise and included in Gross Revenues: any gratuities or service charges added to a customer's bill; any credits or refunds made to customers, guests or patrons; any sums and credits received by the Enterprise for lost or damaged merchandise; any sales taxes, excise taxes, gross receipt taxes, admission taxes, entertainment taxes, tourist taxes or charges received from patrons and passed on to a governmental or quasi-governmental entity; any proceeds from the sale or other disposition of furnishings and equipment or other capital assets; any fire and extended coverage insurance proceeds other than for business interruption; any condemnation awards other than for temporary condemnation; any proceeds of financing or refinancing; and any interest on bank account(s). It is intended that this provision be consistent with 25 U.S.C. 2703(9).

"Net Revenues (Other)" shall mean all Gross Revenues of the Enterprise from all other sources in support of Class II or Class III gaming not included in "Net Revenues (Gaming)," such as food and beverage, entertainment, and retail, less all non-gaming related Operating Expenses, excluding the Management Fee and less the retail value of Promotional

Allowances, if any, and less the following revenues actually received by the Enterprise and included in Gross Revenues: any gratuities or service charges added to a customer's bill; any credits or refunds made to customers, guests or patrons; any sums and credits received by the Enterprise for lost or damaged merchandise; any sales taxes, excise taxes, gross receipt taxes, admission taxes, entertainment taxes, tourist taxes or charges received from patrons and passed on to a governmental or quasi-governmental entity; any proceeds from the sale or other disposition of furnishings and equipment or other capital assets; any fire and extended coverage insurance proceeds other than for business interruption; any condemnation awards other than for temporary condemnation; any proceeds of financing or refinancing; and any interest on bank account(s). It is intended that this provision be consistent with 25 U.S.C. 2703(9).

"Note" shall mean the promissory note or notes to be executed by the Enterprise and/or the Tribe pursuant to the Financing Agreements.

"Operating Budget and Annual Plan" shall mean the operating budget and plan described in Section 3.9.

"Operating Expenses" shall mean all expenses of the operation of the Enterprise, pursuant to GAAP, including but not limited to the following: the payment of salaries, wages, and benefit programs for Enterprise Employees; Operating Supplies for the Enterprise; utilities; repairs and maintenance of the Facility (excluding Capital Replacements); interest on the Note; interest on installment contract purchases or other interest charges on debt approved by the Tribal Council; insurance and bonding; advertising and marketing, including busing and transportation of patrons to the Facility; accounting, legal and other professional fees; security costs; reasonable travel expenses for officers and employees of the Enterprise; lease payments for Furnishings and Equipment to the extent approved by the Tribe; costs of goods sold; other expenses designated as operating Expenses in accordance with the accounting standards as referred to in Section 3.19.3; expenses specifically designated as Operating Expenses in this Agreement; depreciation and amortization of the Facility based on an assumed thirty (30) year life, and depreciation and amortization of all other assets in accordance with GAAP; recruiting and training expenses; fees due to the NIGC under the IGRA; any required payments to the state or local governments made by or on behalf of the Enterprise or the Tribe pursuant to the Compact; license fees reflecting reasonable regulatory costs incurred by the Tribal Gaming Agency; and any budgeted charitable contributions by the Enterprise which are approved by the Tribe.

"Operating Supplies" shall mean food and beverages (alcoholic and nonalcoholic) and other consumable items used in the operation of the Facility, such as playing cards, tokens, chips, pull-tabs, bingo paper, plaques, fuel, soap, cleaning materials, matches, paper goods, stationery and all other similar items.

"Option Date" shall have the meaning described in Section **10.10.**

"Pre-Opening Budget" shall have the meaning described in Section 3.8. "Pre-Opening Expenses" shall have the meaning described in Section 3.8.

"Promotional Allowances" shall mean the retail value of complimentary food, beverages, merchandise, and tokens for gaming, provided to patrons as promotional items.

"Property" shall mean the Tribe's "Indian lands" consisting of approximately of 240 acres of land located at 46-200 Harrison Place, Coachella, Riverside County CA 92236, pursuant to a declaration of trust by the United States of America dated May 18, 1978, recorded June 27, 1978 in the Official Records of Riverside County, California in Book 1978, Page 131619, more specifically described on Exhibit A attached hereto.

"Relative" shall have the meaning described in Section 9.5.

"Shortfall Amount" shall mean any amount necessary to pay Manager all or any portion of the Management Fee due but not paid to Manager as a result of a shortage of available funds.

"State" shall refer to the State of California.

"Term" shall mean the term of this Agreement as described in Section 2.2.

"Transfer and Deposit Agreement" shall mean that certain Transfer and Deposit Agreement dated as of October 17, 2001 between the Enterprise and First National Bank, as Depository.

"Tribal Council" shall mean the duly elected Tribal Council of the Tribe described in the Tribe's Articles of Association.

"Tribal Gaming Authority" shall mean the Tribal body created pursuant to the Tribal Gaming Code to regulate the Class II and Class III Gaming of the Tribe in accordance with the Compact, the IGRA and the Tribal Gaming Code.

"Tribal Gaming Code" shall mean the Gaming Ordinance adopted by the Tribe and approved by the Chairman of the NIGC regulating the conduct of gaming on tribal lands, as amended following the passage of Proposition 1A to permit Class III Gaming at the Facility in accordance with the Compact, together with the Tribal Gaming Commission Rules and Regulations.

"Tribal Priority Distribution" shall mean

"Tribal Resolution" shall have the meaning described in Section 2.9.

SECTION 2
COVENANTS

In consideration of the mutual covenants contained in this Agreement, the parties agree and covenant as follows:

2.1 Engagement of Manager. The Enterprise hereby retains and engages Manager as the exclusive manager of the Enterprise pursuant to the terms and conditions of this Agreement, and Manager hereby accepts such retention and engagement, subject to receipt of all necessary regulatory approvals.

2.2 Term. The management services to be provided under this Agreement shall commence on the Commencement Date, and will terminate on the date which is the [1] anniversary of the Commencement Date. _

Manager shall be granted an additional two (2) year term of this Agreement; provided, however that the NIGC shall first have approved such extension of the term of this Agreement.

2.3 Status of Property. The Tribe represents and covenants that it will maintain the Property throughout the Term as Indian Lands, eligible as a location upon which

Class II and Class III Gaming can occur. The Tribe covenants, during the term hereof, that Manager shall and may peaceably have complete access to and presence in the Facility in accordance with the terms of this Agreement, free from molestation, eviction and disturbance by the Tribe or by any other person or entity; provided, however, that such right of access to and presence in the Facility shall cease (i) in the event the Tribal Gaming Authority revokes any license issued by it to Manager which license is necessary for the lawful operation of the Facility by Manager, or (ii) upon the termination of this Agreement pursuant to its terms.

2.4 Manager Compliance with Law; Licenses. Manager covenants that it will at all times comply with all Legal Requirements, including the Tribal Gaming Code, the IGRA, the Compact, California statutes, to the extent applicable, and any licenses issued under any of the foregoing. The Tribe shall not unreasonably withhold, delay, withdraw, qualify or condition such licenses as the Tribe is authorized to grant.

2.5 Amendments to Tribal Gaming Code. The Tribe covenants that any amendments made to the Tribal Gaming Code will be a legitimate effort to ensure that gaming is conducted in a manner that adequately protects the environment, the public health and safety, and the integrity of the Enterprise. The adoption of any amendments to the Tribal Gaming Code or any other codes or resolutions that would materially and adversely affect Manager's rights under this Agreement shall be a Material Breach of this Agreement.

2.6 Compliance with Compact. The parties shall at all times comply with the provisions of the Compact.

2.7 Fire and Safety. Manager shall ensure that the Facility shall be constructed and maintained in compliance with all fire and safety statutes, codes, and regulations which would be applicable if the Facility were located outside of the jurisdiction of the Tribe although those requirements would not otherwise apply within that jurisdiction. Nothing in this Section shall grant any jurisdiction to the State of California or any political subdivision thereof over the Property or the Facility. The Tribe shall be responsible for arranging fire protection and police services for the Facility.

2.8 Compliance with the National Environmental Policy Act. With the assistance of Manager, the Tribe shall supply the NIGC with all information necessary for the NIGC to comply with any regulations of the NIGC issued pursuant to the National Environmental Policy Act (NEPA).

2.9 Satisfaction of Effective Date Requirements. Manager, the Enterprise and the Tribe each agree to cooperate and to use their best efforts to satisfy all of the conditions of the Effective Date at the earliest possible date. The Tribe shall adopt a resolution (the "Tribal Resolution") reciting that it is the governing law of the Tribe that the Management Agreement, the Financing Agreements and the exhibited documents attached thereto are the legal and binding obligations of the Tribe, valid and enforceable in accordance with their terms. Manager agrees to memorialize the satisfaction of each of the following requirements as well as the Effective Date in writings signed by Manager and delivered to the Tribe and to the Chairman of the NIGC: (i) Manager has satisfied itself as to the proper ownership and control of the Property, and that all of the Legal Requirements and other requirements for lawful conduct and operation of the Facility in accordance with this Agreement have been met and satisfied; and **(ii)** the satisfactory completion of all necessary and applicable feasibility studies required for the operation of the Facility.

2.10 <u>Commencement Date.</u> Manager shall memorialize the Commencement Date in a writing signed by Manager and delivered to the Tribe and to the Chairman of the NIGC.

2.11 <u>Restrictions on Collateral Operations.</u> During the term of this Agreement, Manager agrees that During the term of this Agreement, the Tribe agrees that

SECTION 3
BUSINESS AFFAIRS

3.1 Manager's Authority and Responsibility. Manager shall conduct and direct all business and affairs in connection with the day-to-day operation, management and maintenance of the Facility and the operation of the Enterprise, including the establishment of operating days and hours. It is the parties' intention that the Facility be open twenty-four (24) hours daily, seven (7) days a week. Upon the Commencement Date, Manager shall be deemed to have the necessary power and authority with respect to the Facility to fulfill all of its responsibilities under this Agreement. Nothing herein grants or is intended to grant Manager a titled interest to the Facility or to the Enterprise. Manager hereby accepts such retention and engagement.

The Tribe shall have the sole proprietary interest in and ultimate responsibility for the conduct of all Gaming conducted by the Enterprise, subject to the rights and responsibilities of Manager under this Agreement.

3.2 Duties of Manager. In managing, operating, maintaining and repairing the Facility, Manager's duties shall include, without limitation, the following:

3.2.1 Physical Duties. Manager shall use reasonable measures for the orderly physical administration, management, and operation of the Facility, including without limitation capital improvements, cleaning, painting, decorating, plumbing, carpeting, grounds care and such other maintenance and repair work as is reasonably necessary.

3.2.2 Compliance. Manager shall comply with all duly enacted statutes, regulations and codes of the State, the federal government, the Tribe and the Tribal Gaming Authority.

3.2.3 Required Filings. Manager shall comply with all applicable provisions of the Internal Revenue Code including, but not limited to, the prompt filing of any cash transaction reports and W-2G reports that may be required by the Internal Revenue Service of the United States or under the Compact. Manager shall also comply with all applicable reporting and filing provisions of all other federal, State, and Tribal regulatory agencies.

3.2.4 <u>Contracts in the Name of the Enterprise and at Arm's</u> <u>Length.</u> Contracts for the operations of the Facility shall be entered into in the name of the Enterprise, and signed by the General Manager.

Nothing contained in this section 3.2.4 shall be deemed to be or constitute a waiver of the Tribe's sovereign immunity.

3.2.5 <u>Facility Operating Standards.</u> Manager shall operate the Facility in a proper, efficient and competitive manner in compliance with all applicable provisions of the _ Compact and the standards promulgated by the NIGC at 25 C.F.R. 542.1 *et seq.*, as in effect at any time.

3.3 <u>Security.</u> Manager shall provide for appropriate security for the operation of the Facility. All aspects of the Facility security shall be the responsibility of Manager. All security officers shall be bonded and insured in an amount commensurate with his or her enforcement duties and obligations. The cost of any charge for security and increased public safety services will be an Operating Expense.

3.4 <u>Damage, Condemnation or Impossibility of the Facility.</u> If, during the term of this Agreement, the Facility is damaged or destroyed by fire, war, or other casualty, or by an Act of God, or is taken by condemnation or sold under the threat of condemnation, or if Gaming on the Property is prohibited as a result of a decision of a court of competent jurisdiction or by operation of any applicable legislation, Manager shall have the following options:

3.4.1 <u>Recommencement of Operations.</u> If Gaming on the Property is prohibited by Legal Requirements, Manager shall have the option to continue its interest in this Agreement and, with the approval of the Tribe, to commence or recommence the operation of Gaming at the Facility if, at some point during the Term of this Agreement, such commencement or recommencement shall be legally and commercially feasible.

3.4.2 <u>Repair or Replacement.</u> If the Facility is damaged, destroyed or condemned so that Gaming can no longer be conducted at the Facility, the Facility shall be reconstructed if the insurance or condemnation proceeds are sufficient to restore or replace the Facility to a condition at least comparable to that before the casualty occurred. If Manager elects to reconstruct the Facility and if the insurance proceeds or condemnation awards are insufficient to reconstruct the Facility to such condition, Manager may, in its sole discretion, supply such additional funds as are necessary to reconstruct the Facility to such condition and such funds shall, with the prior consent of the Tribe and the BIA or NIGC, as appropriate, constitute a loan to the Enterprise, secured by the revenues from the Facility and repayable upon such terms as may be agreed upon by the Enterprise and Manager. If the insurance proceeds are not sufficient and are not used to repair the Facility, the Enterprise and Manager shall jointly adjust and settle any and all claims for such insurance proceeds or condemnation awards, and such proceeds or award shall be applied first, to the amounts due under the Note (including principal and interest); second, any other loans; third, any undistributed Net Revenues pursuant to Section 5 of this Agreement; and fourth, any surplus shall be distributed to the Tribe.

3.4.3 <u>Other Business Purposes.</u> Manager shall have the option to use the Facility for other purposes reasonably incidental to Class II and Class III Gaming, provided the Enterprise has approved such purposes (which approval shall not be unreasonably withheld). For any purpose other than Gaming, Manager shall obtain all approvals necessary under applicable law.

3.4.4 <u>Termination of Gaming.</u> Manager shall have the option at any time within a sixty (60) day period following the cessation of Gaming on the Property to notify the Enterprise in writing that it is terminating operations under this Agreement, in which case Manager shall retain any rights Manager may have to undistributed Net Revenues pursuant to Section 5 of this Agreement and rights to repayments of amounts owed to it. If Manager does not elect to terminate this Agreement, it may take whatever action may be necessary to reduce expenses during such termination of Gaming.

3.4.5 <u>Tolling of the Agreement.</u> If, after a period of cessation of Gaming on the Property, the recommencement of Gaming is possible, and if Manager has not terminated this Agreement under the provisions of Section 3.4.4, the period of such cessation shall not be deemed to have been part of the term of this Agreement and the date of expiration of the term of this Agreement shall be extended by the number of days of such cessation period.

3.5 <u>Alcoholic Beverages and Tobacco Sales.</u> No Tribal legislation prohibiting the sale of tobacco and/or alcoholic beverages is now in force, and no such legislation will be enacted during the term of this Agreement. The Tribe agrees to enact any Tribal legislation necessary to allow sale of alcoholic beverages or tobacco products in the facility. The Enterprise and Manager mutually agree to include sale of tobacco and alcoholic beverages within the Facility to the fullest extent allowed by the Compact.

3.6 <u>Employees.</u>

3.6.1 <u>Manager's Responsibility.</u> Manager shall have, subject to the terms of this Agreement, the exclusive responsibility and authority to direct the selection, control and discharge of all employees performing regular services for the Enterprise in connection with the maintenance, operation, and management of the Facility and any activity upon the Property; and the sole responsibility for determining whether a prospective employee is qualified and the appropriate level of compensation to be paid; provided, however, the Tribal Gaming Authority shall have sole and exclusive control over the licensing of employees or prospective employees of the Enterprise, and the compliance by such employees with the conditions of their license.

3.6.2 <u>Enterprise Employee Policies.</u> Manager shall prepare a draft of personnel policies and procedures (the "Enterprise Employee Policies"), including a job classification system with salary levels and scales, which policies and procedures shall be subject to approval by the Enterprise. The Enterprise Employee Policies shall include a grievance procedure in order to establish fair and uniform standards for the employees of the Enterprise, which will include procedures for the resolution of disputes between Manager and Enterprise Employees. Any revisions to the Enterprise Employee Policies shall not be effective unless they are approved in the same manner as the original Enterprise Employee Policies. All such actions shall comply with applicable Tribal law.

3.6.3 <u>Employees.</u> The selection by the Manager of the General Manager, Chief Financial Officer, Director of Human Resources and Public Safety Director of the Enterprise shall be subject to the approval of the Enterprise, which approval shall not be unreasonably withheld. Manager shall provide the Tribal Council with sufficient information to adequately evaluate all recommendations for employment in the positions of General Manager, Chief Financial Officer, or Security Director. The terms of employment of the Enterprise Employees shall be structured as though all labor, employment, and unemployment insurance laws applicable in California employees would also apply to Enterprise Employees. The Enterprise agrees to take no action to impede, supersede or impair such treatment.

3.6.4 Off-Site Employees. Subject to approval of the Enterprise, Manager shall also have the right to use employees of Manager and Manager's Affiliates not located at the Facility to provide services to the Enterprise ("Off-Site Employees"). All expenses, costs (including, but not limited to, salaries and benefits, but excluding pension, retirement, severance or similar benefits), which are related to such Off-Site Employees shall be paid by Manager.

3.6.5 No Manager Wages or Salaries. Neither Manager nor Manager's Affiliates nor any of their officers, directors, shareholders, or employees shall be compensated by wages from or contract payments by the Enterprise for their efforts or for any work which they perform under this Agreement, other than repayments of advances and the Management Fee to be paid to Manager under Section 5.1. Nothing in this subsection shall restrict the ability of an employee of the Enterprise to purchase or hold stock in Manager, or Manager's Affiliates where (i) such stock is publicly held, and (ii) such employee acquires, on a cumulative basis, less than five (5%) percent of the outstanding stock in the corporation.

3.6.6 Employee Background Checks. A background investigation shall be conducted by the Tribal Gaming Authority in compliance with all Legal Requirements, to the extent applicable, on each applicant for employment as soon as reasonably practicable, and in all events within the time necessary to enable the Tribal Gaming Authority to forward a report on such applicant for employment pursuant to 25 C.F.R. 556.5(b) within the 60 day time period provided in 25 C.F.R. 558.3(b). No individual whose prior activities, criminal record, if any, or reputation, habits and associations are known to pose a threat to the public interest, the effective regulation of Gaming, or to the gaming licenses of Manager or any of its Affiliates, or to create or enhance the dangers of unsuitable, unfair or illegal practices and methods and activities in the conduct of Gaming, shall knowingly be employed by Manager, the Enterprise, or the Tribe.

The background investigation procedures employed by the Tribal Gaming Authority shall be formulated in consultation with Manager and shall satisfy all regulatory requirements independently applicable to Manager and its Affiliates. Any cost associated with obtaining background investigations of the Manager, the Enterprise, or the Tribe for the Tribal Gaming Authority shall constitute an Operating Expense; costs associated with obtaining background investigations of Manager for the NIGC shall be paid by Manager.

3.6.7 Indian Preference, Recruiting and Training. Manager shall offer employment in the Enterprise to all employees in good standing of the Class II gaming facility operated by the Tribe prior to the Commencement Date. For additional employment needs, Manager shall, during the term of this Agreement, to the extent permitted by applicable law, including but not limited to the Indian Civil Rights Act, 25 U.S.C. 1301 *et seq.*, and the Compact, give preference in recruiting, training and employment to qualified members of a Native American Tribe recognized by the Federal government or the State of California, their spouses and children in all job categories of the Enterprise. Manager shall: conduct job fairs and skills assessment meetings for Native Americans; abide by any duly enacted Tribal preference laws; in consultation with and subject to the approval of the Tribe, develop a management training program for Native Americans. This program shall be structured to provide appropriate training for those participating to assume full managerial control at the conclusion of the Term of this Agreement; train and hire, to the maximum extent permitted by law, members of the local communities where the Facility is located. Whenever possible, Enterprise jobs shall be filled by Native Americans and persons living within Riverside County. Final determination of the qualifications of Native Americans and all other persons for employment shall be made by Manager, subject to any licensing requirements of the Tribe Gaming Authority.

3.6.8 Goals and Remedies. All hiring for the Enterprise shall be done by Manager, based on the hiring policies established by the Enterprise in consultation with Manager.

3.6.9 Removal of Employees. Manager will act in accordance with the Enterprise Employee Policies with respect to the discharge, demotion or discipline of any Enterprise Employee.

3.7 Marketing.

3.7.1 Nature of Marketing Services. The services described in this Section 3.7 ("Marketing Services") shall be provided by Manager.

3.7.2 Marketing Services. Manager shall provide the following Marketing Services:

3.8 Pre-Opening. Upon the later of (a) six (6) months prior to the scheduled Commencement Date and (b) fifteen (15) days following the Effective Date, Manager shall commence implementation of a pre-opening program which shall include all activities necessary to financially and operationally prepare the Facility for opening. To implement the pre-opening program, Manager shall prepare a comprehensive pre-opening budget which shall be submitted to the Enterprise for its approval upon the later of (x) seven (7) months prior to the scheduled Commencement Date and (y) fifteen (15) days following the Effective Date ("Pre-Opening Budget"). The Pre-Opening Budget sets forth expenses which Manager anticipates to be necessary or desirable in order to prepare the Facility for the Commencement Date, including without limitation,

The Enterprise agrees that the Pre-Opening Budget may be modified from time to time, subject to approval of the Enterprise in accordance with the procedure established by Article 3.9 of this Agreement for adjustments to the Operating Budget and Annual Plan.

3.9 Operating Budget and Annual Plan. Manager shall, prior to the scheduled Commencement Date, submit to the Enterprise, for its approval, a proposed Operating Budget and Annual Plan for the remainder of the current Fiscal Year. Thereafter, Manager shall, not less than sixty (60) days prior to the commencement of each full or partial Fiscal Year, submit to the Enterprise, for its approval, a proposed Operating Budget and Annual Plan for the ensuing full or partial Fiscal Year, as the case may be. The Operating Budget and Annual Plan shall include

The Operating Budget and Annual Plan for the Facility will be comprised of the following:

The Enterprise's approval of the Operating Budget and Annual Plan shall not be unreasonably withheld or delayed. Manager shall meet with the Enterprise to discuss the proposed Operating Budget and Annual Plan and the Enterprise's approval shall be deemed given unless a specific written objection thereto is delivered by the Enterprise to Manager within thirty (30) days after Manager and the Enterprise have met to discuss the proposed Operating Budget and Annual Plan. If the Enterprise for any reason shall fail to meet with Manager to discuss a proposed Operating Budget and Annual Plan, the Enterprise shall be deemed to have consented unless a specific written objection is delivered to Manager within fifteen (15) days after the date the proposed Operating Budget and Annual Plan is submitted to the Enterprise. The Enterprise shall review the Operating Budget and Annual Plan on a line-by-line basis. To be effective, any notice which disapproves a proposed Operating Budget and Annual Plan must contain specific objections in reasonable detail to individual line items.

If the initial proposed Operating Budget and Annual Plan contains any disputed budget item(s), the Enterprise and Manager agree to cooperate with each other in good faith to resolve the disputed or objectionable proposed item(s). In the event the Enterprise and Manager are not able to reach mutual agreement concerning any disputed or objectionable item(s) prior to the commencement of the applicable fiscal year, the undisputed portions of the proposed Operating Budget and Annual Plan shall be deemed to be adopted and approved and the corresponding line item(s) contained in the Operating Budget and Annual Plan for the preceding fiscal year shall be adjusted as set forth herein and shall be substituted in lieu of the disputed item(s) in the proposed Operating Budget and Annual Plan. Those line items which are in dispute shall be determined by

The resulting Operating Budget and Annual Plan obtained in accordance with the preceding sentence shall be deemed to be the Operating Budget and Annual Plan in effect until such time as

Manager and the Enterprise have resolved the items objected to by the Enterprise.

3.9.1 <u>Adjustments to Operating Budget and Annual Plan.</u> Manager may, after notice to and approval by the Enterprise, revise the Operating Budget and Annual Plan from time to time, as necessary, to reflect any unpredicted significant changes, variables or events or to include additional, unanticipated items of expense. Manager may, after notice to the Enterprise, reallocate part or all of the amount budgeted with respect to any line item to another line item and to make such other modifications to the Operating Budget and Annual Plan as

Manager deems necessary, provided that the total adjustments to the Operating Budget and Annual Plan shall not exceed one hundred ten percent (110%) of the aggregate approved Operating Budget and Annual Plan without approval of the Enterprise. Manager shall submit a revision of the Operating Budget and Annual Plan to the Tribe for review on a quarterly basis. In addition, in the event actual Gross Revenues for any period are greater than those provided for in the Operating Budget and Annual Plan, the amounts approved in the Operating Budget and Annual Plan for guest services, food and beverage, telephone, utilities, marketing and the repair and maintenance of the Facility for any month shall be automatically deemed to be increased to an amount that bears the same relationship (ratio) to the amounts budgeted for such items as actual Gross Revenue for such month bears to the projected Gross Revenue for such month. The Enterprise acknowledges that the Operating Budget and Annual Plan is intended only to be a reasonable estimate of the Facility's revenues and expenses for the ensuing Fiscal Year.

Manager shall not be deemed to have made any guarantee concerning projected results contained in the Operating Budget and Annual Plan.

3.10 <u>Capital Budgets; Permitted Hotel Debt.</u> Manager shall, prior to the Commencement Date and thereafter, not less than sixty (60) days prior to the commencement of each fiscal year, or partial fiscal year after the Commencement Date, submit to the Enterprise a recommended capital budget (the "Capital Budget")

describing the present value, estimated useful life and estimated
replacement costs for the ensuing full or partial year, as the case
may be, for the physical plant, furnishings, equipment, and
ordinary capital replacement items, all of which are defined to be
any items, the cost of which is capitalized and depreciated, rather
than expensed, using GAAP ("Capital Replacements") as shall
be required to operate the Facility in accordance with sound
business practices.

The Enterprise and Manager shall meet to discuss the proposed
Capital Budget and the Enterprise shall be required to make
specific written objections to a proposed Capital Budget in the
same manner and within the same time periods specified in
Section 3.9 with respect to an Operating Budget and Annual Plan.
The Enterprise shall not unreasonably withhold or delay its
consent. Unless the Enterprise and Manager otherwise agree,
Manager shall be responsible for

3.11 Capital Replacements. The Enterprise shall effect and
expend such amounts for any Capital Replacements as shall be
required, in the course of the operation of the Facility, to
maintain, at a minimum, the Facility in compliance with any
Legal Requirements and to comply with Manager's recommended
programs for renovation, modernization and improvement
intended to keep the Facility competitive in its market, to
maintain industry standards; or to correct any condition of an
emergency nature, including without limitation, maintenance,
replacements or repairs which are required to be effected by the
Enterprise, which in Manager's sole discretion requires immediate
action to preserve and protect the Facility, assure its continued
operation, and/or protect the comfort, health, safety and/or
welfare of the Facility's guests or employees (an "Emergency
Condition"); provided, however, that the Enterprise shall be
under no obligation to fund Capital Replacements in aggregate
amount greater than its periodic required contributions to the
Capital Replacement Reserve described in Section 3.12. Manager
is authorized to take all steps and to make all expenditures from
the Working Capital Account, described at Section 3.17.1 (in the
case of non-capitalized repairs and maintenance), or Capital

Replacement Reserve Account, described at Section 3.12, (in the case of expenditures for Capital Replacements) as it deems necessary to repair and correct any Emergency Condition, regardless whether such provisions have been made in the Capital Budget or the Operating Budget and Annual Plan for any such expenditures; or the cost thereof may be advanced by Manager and reimbursed from future revenues. Design and installation of Capital Replacements shall be effected in a time period and subject to such conditions as the Enterprise may establish to minimize interference with or disruption of ongoing operations.

3.12 Capital Replacement Reserve. Manager shall establish a Capital Replacement Reserve on the books of account of the Facility, and an account (the "Capital Replacement Reserve Account") in the Enterprise's name at a bank designated by the Enterprise in accordance with Section 3.17A of this Agreement.

3.13 Periodic Contributions to Capital Replacement Reserve. In accordance with Section 5.4 of this Agreement, Manager shall make monthly deposits into the Capital Replacement Reserve Account in amounts equivalent to if any adjustment of Net Revenues is made as a result of an audit or for other accounting reasons, a corresponding adjustment in the Capital Replacement Reserve Account deposit shall be made. In addition, all proceeds from the sale of capital items no longer needed for the operation of the Facility, and the proceeds of any insurance received in reimbursement for any items previously paid for from the Capital Replacement Reserve, shall be deposited into the Capital Replacement Reserve Account upon receipt.

3.14 Use and Allocation of Capital Replacement Reserve. Any expenditures for Capital Replacements which have been budgeted and previously approved may be paid from the Capital Replacement Reserve Account without further approval from the Enterprise. Any amounts remaining in the Capital Replacement Reserve Account at the close of any year shall be carried forward and retained in the Capital Replacement Reserve Account until fully used. If amounts in the Capital Replacement Reserve Account at the end of any year plus the anticipated contributions to the Capital Replacement Reserve Account for the next ensuing year are not sufficient to pay for Capital Replacements authorized by the Capital Budget for such ensuing year, then funds in the amount of the projected deficiency may be advanced by Manager to be repaid to Manager pursuant to Section 5.4 of this Agreement as a Manager Advance.

3.15 Contracting. In entering contracts for the supply of goods and services for the Facility, Manager shall give preference to qualified members of the Tribe, their spouses and children, and qualified business entities certified by the Tribe to be controlled by members of the Tribe.

"Qualified" shall mean a member of the Tribe, a member's spouse or children, or a business entity certified by the Tribe to be controlled by members of the Tribe, who or which is able to provide services at competitive prices, has demonstrated skills and abilities to perform the tasks to be undertaken in an acceptable manner, in Manager's opinion, and can meet the reasonable bonding and/or financial requirements of Manager.

3.16 Internal Control Systems. Manager shall install systems for monitoring of all funds (the "Internal Control Systems"), which systems shall comply with all Legal Requirements, and shall be submitted to the Enterprise and the Tribal Gaming Authority for approval in advance of implementation, which approval shall not be unreasonably withheld. The Enterprise shall have the right to retain an auditor to review the adequacy of the Internal Control Systems prior to the Commencement Date. If the Enterprise elects to exercise this right, the cost of such review shall be a Pre-Opening Expense. Any significant changes in such systems after the Commencement Date also shall be subject to review and approval by the Tribal Gaming Authority in advance of implementation. The Tribal Gaming Authority and Manager shall have the right and duty to maintain and police the Internal Control Systems in order to prevent any loss of proceeds from the Facility. The Tribal Gaming Authority shall have the right to inspect and oversee the Internal Control System at all times. Manager shall install a closed circuit television system to be used for monitoring all cash handling activities of the Facility sufficient to meet all Legal Requirements.

3.17 <u>Banking and Bank Accounts.</u>

3.17.1 <u>Enterprise Bank Accounts.</u> The Enterprise shall select a bank or banks for the deposit and maintenance of funds and shall establish in such bank or banks accounts as Manager deems appropriate and necessary in the course of business and as consistent with this Agreement, including, but not limited to, a Depository Account, Disbursement Account, a Working Capital Account and a Capital Replacement Reserve Account ("Enterprise Bank Accounts"). Establishment of any Enterprise Bank Account shall be subject to the approval of the Enterprise. The sum of money agreed upon by the Manager and the Enterprise to be maintained in the Working Capital Account to serve as working capital for Facility operations, shall include

Attached hereto as Exhibit E is the form of Irrevocable Banking Instructions to be executed by the Enterprise with regard to each Enterprise Bank Account and to be in effect during the Term of this Agreement, other than with respect to the accounts maintained by the Enterprise with the "Collection Bank" and the "Depository Bank" pursuant to the Transfer and Deposit Agreement.

The parties agree that so long as the Transfer and Deposit Agreement shall be in effect, the "Accounts" specified therein shall constitute the Disbursement Account of the Enterprise.

3.17.2 <u>Daily Deposits to Depository Account.</u> Manager shall

3.17.3 <u>Disbursement Account.</u> Manager shall, consistent with and pursuant to the approved annual Operating Budget and Annual Plan, have responsibility and authority for making or otherwise authorizing all payments for Operating Expenses, debt service, Management Fees, and disbursements to the Tribe from the Disbursement Account in accordance with the provisions of Section 5.

3.17.4 Transfers Between Accounts. Manager has the authority to

3.18 <u>Insurance.</u> Manager, on behalf of the Tribe and the Enterprise, shall arrange for, obtain and maintain, or cause its agents to maintain, with responsible insurance carriers licensed to do business in the State of California, insurance satisfactory to

Manager and the Enterprise covering the Facility and the operations of the Enterprise, naming the Tribe, the Enterprise, Manager, and Manager's Affiliates as insured parties, in at least the amounts which are set forth in Exhibit F.

3.19 Accounting and Books of Account.

3.19.1 Statements. Manager shall prepare and provide operating statements to the Enterprise on a monthly, quarterly, and annual basis. The operating statements shall comply with all Legal Requirements and shall include an income statement, statement of cash flows, and balance sheet for the Enterprise. Such statements shall include the Operating Budget and Annual Plan and Capital Budget projections as comparative statements, and which, after the first full year of operation, will include comparative statements from the comparable period for the prior year of all revenues, and all other amounts collected and received, and all deductions and disbursements made therefrom in connection with the Facility.

3.19.2 Books of Account. Manager shall maintain full and accurate books of account at an office in the Facility. The Enterprise and the Tribe shall have the right to immediate access to the daily operations of the Facility and shall have the unlimited right to inspect, examine, and copy all such books and supporting business records. Any such copies are to be considered confidential and proprietary and shall not be divulged to any third parties without the express written permission of the Enterprise. Such rights may be exercised through the Tribal Gaming Agency or through an agent, employee, attorney, or independent accountant acting on behalf of the Tribe or the Enterprise.

3.19.3 Accounting Standards. Manager shall maintain the books and records reflecting the operations of the Facility in accordance with the accounting practices of Manager in conformity with Generally Accepted Accounting Principles consistently applied and shall adopt and follow the fiscal accounting periods utilized by Manager in its normal course of business (i.e., a month, quarter and year prepared in accordance with the Enterprise Fiscal Year). The accounting systems and procedures shall comply with Legal Requirements and, at a minimum: include an adequate system of internal accounting controls; permit the preparation of financial statements in accordance with generally accepted accounting principles; be susceptible to audit; permit the calculation and payment of the Management Fee described in Section 5; provide for the allocation of operating expenses or overhead expenses among the Tribe, the Enterprise, and any other user of shared facilities and services; and (vi) allow the Enterprise, the Tribe and the NIGC to calculate the annual fees required under 25 C.F.R. 514.1.

3.19.4 Annual Audit. An independent certified public accounting firm of national recognition engaged by the Enterprise or the Tribe shall perform an annual audit of the books and records of the Enterprise and of all contracts for supplies, services or concessions reflecting Operating Expenses. The BIA and the NIGC shall also have the right to perform special audits of the Enterprise on any aspect of the Enterprise at any time without restriction. The costs incurred for such audits shall constitute an Operating Expense. Such audits shall be provided by the Tribe or the Enterprise, as the case may be, to all applicable federal and state agencies, as required by law, and may be used by Manager for reporting purposes under federal and state securities laws, if required.

3.20 Retail Shops and Concessions. With respect to the operation of the shops and concessions located within the Facility, the Enterprise shall approve in advance in writing the specific type or types of shops or concessions proposed by Manager to be authorized for inclusion in the Facility.

SECTION 4
LIENS

4.1 Liens. Subject to the exceptions hereinafter stated in Section 5.1, the Tribe and the Enterprise specifically warrant and represent to Manager that during the term of this Agreement neither the Tribe nor the Enterprise shall act in any way whatsoever, either directly or indirectly, to cause any person or entity to become an encumbrancer or lienholder of the Property or the Facility, other than the Lender, or to allow any person or entity to obtain any interest in this Agreement without the prior written consent of Manager, and, where applicable, consent from the United States. Manager specifically warrants and represents to the Tribe and the Enterprise that during the term of this Agreement Manager shall not act in any way, directly or indirectly, to cause any person or entity to become an encumbrancer or lienholder of the Property or the Facility, or to obtain any interest in this Agreement without the prior written consent of the Tribe or the Enterprise, and, where applicable, the United States. The Tribe, the Enterprise and Manager shall keep the Facility and Property free and clear of all enforceable mechanics' and other enforceable liens resulting from the construction of the Facility and all other enforceable liens which may attach to the Facility or the Property, which shall at all times remain the property of the United States in trust for the Tribe. If any such lien is claimed or filed, it shall be the duty of Manager, utilizing funds of the Enterprise, to discharge the lien within thirty (30) days after having been given written notice of such claim, either by payment to the claimant, by the posting of a bond and the payment into the court of the amount necessary to relieve and discharge the Property from such claim, or in any other manner which will result in the discharge or stay of such claim.

4.2 Exceptions. The Enterprise shall have the right to grant security interests in Facility revenues, as well as first priority security interests in any Facility assets other than personal property purchased with the proceeds of the Loan, but only if such security interests are granted to secure loans made to and for the benefit of the Enterprise.

SECTION 5
MANAGEMENT FEE, REIMBURSEMENTS
AND DISBURSEMENTS BY MANAGER

5.1 **Management Fee.** In consideration of the services rendered by Manager pursuant to this Agreement, Manager shall be entitled to an annual Management Fee equal to The Management Fee shall be payable monthly in an amount equal to the accrued Management Fee for the preceding month plus any Shortfall Amount. Notwithstanding anything contained in this Agreement to the contrary, Manager shall not be entitled to any compensation for providing management services pursuant to this Agreement other than the annual Management Fee.

5.2 **Disbursements for Operating Expenses.** Each month, Manager shall, for and on behalf of the Enterprise, cause funds to be disbursed from the Disbursement Account, to the extent available, to pay Operating Expenses due and payable. So long as the Transfer and Deposit Agreement shall be in effect, such disbursements shall be from the "Operating Account" specified therein.

5.3 **Disbursements for Debt Service.** After the disbursements pursuant to Section 5.2, Manager shall, for and on behalf of the Enterprise, disburse funds from the Disbursement Account, to the extent available, to pay debt service due and payable in accordance with the Loan Agreement. Thereafter, Manager shall, for and on behalf of the Enterprise, cause funds to be disbursed from the Disbursement Account, to the extent available, to pay debt service due and payable in accordance with Financing Agreements other than the Loan Agreement in accordance with the payment priorities specified in the Loan Agreement and the Financing Agreements. So long as the Transfer and Deposit Agreement shall be in effect, such disbursements shall be from the "Debt Service Account," "Permitted Equipment Debt Account," and "Permitted Other Debt Account" specified therein, respectively.

5.4 **Payment of Fees and Tribal Disbursement.** Within twenty-one (21) days after the end of each calendar month of operations, Manager shall calculate Gross Revenues, Operating Expenses, and Net Revenues of the Facility for the previous month's operations and the year's operations to date.

5.4.1 <u>Disbursements Pursuant to Transfer and Deposit Agreement.</u> After the disbursements pursuant to Sections 5.2 and 5.3, so long as the Transfer and Deposit Agreement shall be in effect, Manager shall cause funds to be disbursed from the Enterprise Bank Account(s) in accordance with the provisions of Section 3.6, 3.7 and 3.8 thereof.

(iv) the balance of Excess Funds shall be disbursed to the Enterprise.

5.4.2 <u>Disbursements Other Than Pursuant to Transfer and Deposit Agreement.</u> In the event the Transfer and Deposit Agreement shall no longer be in effect, after the disbursements pursuant to Sections 5.2 and 5.3, Manager shall cause the funds remaining in the Enterprise Bank Account(s) ("Excess Funds") to be applied in the following order:

5.4.3 <u>Shortfall Amounts and Manager Advances.</u> Shortfall Amounts due Manager and Manager Advances shall be paid at such time as sufficient Excess Funds exist to pay such Shortfall Amounts or Manager Advances in accordance with Section 5.4,

5.5 <u>Minimum Guaranteed Monthly Payment.</u> Manager shall pay the Tribe from Net Revenues per month (the "Minimum Guaranteed *1q* Monthly Payment"), beginning on the Commencement Date and continuing for the remainder of the Term in accordance with Section 5.4. The Minimum Guaranteed Monthly Payment shall have preference over the retirement of development and construction costs of the Facility. The Minimum Guaranteed Monthly Payment shall be payable to the Tribe in arrears on the twenty-first (21') day of each calendar month following the month in which the Commencement Date occurs, which payment shall have priority over the Management Fee. If the Commencement Date is a date other than the first day of a calendar month, the first payment will be prorated from the Commencement Date to the end of the month. Minimum Guaranteed Monthly Payments shall be charged against the Tribe's distribution of Net Revenues for each month provided, however,

In the event Class II and/or Class III gaming is suspended for any portion of a month, the Guaranteed Monthly Payment shall be prorated and payable for the portion of the month during which gaming was conducted at the Facility. No Minimum Guaranteed

Monthly Payment shall be owed for a month in the event Class II and/or Class III gaming is suspended or terminated at the Facility pursuant to Section 3.4 for the entire month. The obligation of Manager to make Minimum Guaranteed Monthly Payments shall cease upon termination of this Agreement. Except as provided in the preceding sentence of this Section 5.5, Manager's obligation to pay the Tribe the Minimum Guaranteed Monthly Payment is unconditional, and shall not be affected by the actual level of funds generated by the Facility.

5.6 Distribution of Excess Funds. The distributions of Excess Funds to the Enterprise pursuant to this Section 5 shall be deposited in the Enterprise's bank account specified by the Enterprise in a notice to Manager pursuant to Section 8.2.

5.7 Manager Guaranty. Manager shall

5.8 Development and Construction Costs. Manager and the Tribe agree that

SECTION 6
TRADE NAMES, TRADE MARKS
AND SERVICE MARKS

6.1 <u>Facility Name.</u> The Facility shall be operated under the name "Trump Spotlight 29 Casino Hotel" or such other name as the parties may agree upon (the "Facility Name") during the Term of this Agreement, subject to and in accordance with the terms and conditions of the Trademark License Agreement dated May 31, 2000, between Trump Hotels & Casino Resorts Holdings, L.P. and the Tribe, as amended by the First Amendment to Trademark License Agreement dated as of March, 2002.

6.2 <u>Signs.</u> Prior to the Commencement Date and from time to time during the Term hereof, Manager agrees to erect and install, in accordance with local codes and regulations, all signs Manager deems necessary in, on or about the Facility, including, but not limited to, signs bearing the Facility Name.

SECTION 7
TAXES

7.1 State and Local Taxes. If the State of California or any local government attempts to impose any tax including any possessory interest tax upon any party to this Agreement or upon the Enterprise, the Facility or the Property, the Tribal Council, in the name of the appropriate party or parties in interest, may resist such attempt through legal action. The costs of such action and the compensation of legal counsel shall be an Operating Expense of the Facility. Any such tax shall constitute an Operating Expense of the Facility. This Section shall in no manner be construed to imply that any party to this Agreement or the Enterprise is liable for any such tax.

7.2 Tribal Taxes. The Tribe agrees that neither it nor any agent, agency, affiliate or representative of the Tribe will impose any taxes, fees, assessments, or other charges of any nature whatsoever on payments of any debt service to Manager or any of its Affiliates or to any lender furnishing financing for the Facility or for the Enterprise, or on the Enterprise, the Facility, the revenues therefrom or on the Management Fee as described in Section 5.1 of this Agreement; provided, however, the Tribe may assess license fees reflecting reasonable regulatory costs incurred by the Tribal Gaming Agency to the extent not paid as Operating Expenses; the Tribe further agrees that neither it nor any agent, agency, affiliate or representative will impose any taxes, fees, assessments or other charges of any nature whatsoever on the salaries or benefits, or dividends paid to, any of Manager's stockholders, officers, directors, or employees, any of the employees of the Enterprise; or any provider of goods, materials, or services to the Facility, other than with respect to any such provider of goods, materials, or services to the Facility, license fees reflecting reasonable regulatory costs incurred by the Tribal Gaming Authority.

Nothing in this Section 7.2 shall be construed to prohibit the Tribe from taxing the sale of goods at the Facility in amounts equivalent to any state taxes that would otherwise be applicable but for the Tribe's status as an Indian Tribe; provided that no such tax shall be applied to any goods supplied as Promotional Allowances.

7.3 Compliance with Internal Revenue Code. Manager shall comply with all applicable provisions of the Internal Revenue Code.

SECTION 8
GENERAL PROVISIONS

8.1 <u>Situs of the Contracts.</u> This Agreement, as well as all contracts entered into between the Tribe, the Enterprise and any person or any entity providing services to the Facility, shall be deemed entered into in California, and shall be subject to all Legal Requirements of the Tribe and federal law as well as approval by the Secretary of the Interior where required by 25 U.S.C. 81 or by the Chairman of the NIGC where required by the IGRA.

8.2 <u>Notice.</u> Any notice required to be given pursuant to this Agreement shall be delivered to the appropriate party by Federal Express or by Certified Mail Return Receipt Requested, addressed as follows:

If to the Tribe or the Enterprise, to:

Dean Mike, Chairman

Twenty-Nine Palms Band of Luiseno Mission Indians of California

46-200 Harrison Place

Coachella CA 92236

with a copy to: Gene R. Gambale, Esq.

Vice President-General Counsel

Spotlight 29 Enterprises

46-200 Harrison Place Coachella CA 92236

If to Manager, to: Robert M. Pickus

Executive Vice President and General Counsel Trump Hotels & Casino Resorts, Inc.

Huron Avenue & Brigantine Boulevard

Atlantic City NJ 08401

with copies to: John M. Peebles, Esq.

Monteau, Peebles & Marks, L.L.P. 12100 West Center Road, Suite 202 Bel Air Plaza

Omaha NE 68144-3960

and: Peter Michael Laughlin, Esq.

Graham, Curtin & Sheridan, PA

4 Headquarters Plaza

Morristown NJ 07962-1991or to such other different address(s) as Manager, the Enterprise or the Tribe may specify in writing using the notice procedure called for in this Section 8.2. Any such notice shall be deemed given two (2) days following deposit in the United States mail or upon actual delivery, whichever first occurs.

8.3 Authority to Execute and Perform Agreement. The Tribe, the Enterprise and Manager represent and warrant to each other that they each have full power and authority to execute this Agreement and to be bound by and perform the terms hereof. On request, each party shall furnish the other evidence of such authority.

8.4 Relationship. Manager, the Enterprise and the Tribe shall not be construed as joint venturers or partners of each other by reason of this Agreement and neither shall have the power to bind or obligate the other except as set forth in this Agreement.

8.5 Manager's Contractual Authority. Manager is authorized to make, enter into and perform in the name of and for the account of the Enterprise, such contracts deemed necessary by Manager to perform its obligations under this Agreement, provided such contracts comply with the terms and conditions of this Agreement, including, but not limited to, Section 3.2.4, and provided such contracts do not obligate the Enterprise to pay sums not approved in the Operating Budget and Annual Plan or the Capital Budget.

8.6 Further Actions. The Tribe, the Enterprise and 'Manager agree to execute all contracts, agreements and documents and to take all actions necessary to comply with the provisions of this Agreement and the intent hereof.

8.7 Defense. Except for disputes between the Tribe, the Enterprise and Manager, and claims relating to the Tribe's status as a Tribe or the trust status of the Property, Manager shall bring and/or defend and/or settle any claim or legal action brought against Manager, the Enterprise or the Tribe, individually, jointly or severally, or any Enterprise Employee, in connection with the operation of the Facility. Subject to the Tribe's approval of legal counsel, Manager shall retain and supervise legal counsel, accountants and such other professionals, consultants and specialists as Manager deems appropriate to defend any such claim or cause of action. All liabilities, costs and expenses, including reasonable attorneys' fees and disbursements incurred in defending and/or settling any such claim or legal action which are not covered by insurance, shall be an Operating Expense. Nothing contained herein is a grant to Manager of the right to waive the Tribe's or the Enterprise's sovereign immunity. That right is strictly reserved to the Tribe and the Enterprise. Any settlement of a third party claim or cause of action shall require approval of the Enterprise.

8.8 <u>Waivers.</u> No failure or delay by Manager, the Enterprise or the Tribe to insist upon the strict performance of any covenant, agreement, term or condition of this Agreement, or to exercise any right or remedy consequent upon the breach thereof, shall constitute a waiver of any such breach or any subsequent breach of such covenant, agreement, term or condition. No covenant, agreement, term, or condition of this Agreement and no breach thereof shall be waived, altered or modified except by written instrument. No waiver of any breach shall affect or alter this Agreement, but each and every covenant, agreement, term and condition of this Agreement shall continue in full force and effect with respect to any other then existing or subsequent breach thereof.

8.9 <u>Captions.</u> The captions for each Section and Subsection are intended for convenience only.

8.10 <u>Severability.</u> If any of the terms and provisions hereof shall be held invalid or unenforceable, such invalidity or unenforceability shall not affect any of the other terms or provisions hereof. If, however, any material part of a party's rights under this Agreement shall be declared invalid or unenforceable, (specifically including Manager's right to receive its Management Fees) the party whose rights have been declared invalid or unenforceable shall have the option to terminate this Agreement upon thirty (30) days written notice to the other party, without liability on the part of the terminating party.

8.11 <u>Interest.</u> Any amounts advanced by Manager related to the operation of the Facility shall accrue interest at the rate specified in the Note; provided, however, no interest shall accrue or be payable in respect of the Minimum Guaranteed Monthly Payment funded by Manager.

8.12 Travel and Out-of-Pocket Expenses. Subject to the Operating Budget and Annual Plan, all travel and out-of-pocket expenses of Enterprise Employees reasonably incurred in the performance of their duties shall be an Operating Expense.

8.13 Third Party Beneficiary. This Agreement is exclusively for the benefit of the parties hereto and it may not be enforced by any party other than the parties to this Agreement and shall not give rise to liability to any third party other than the authorized successors and assigns of the parties hereto as such are authorized by this Agreement.

8.14 Brokerage. Manager, the Enterprise and the Tribe represent and warrant to each other that none of them has sought the services of a broker, finder or agent in this transaction, and none of them has employed, nor authorized, any other person to act in such capacity. Manager, the Enterprise and the Tribe each hereby agrees to indemnify and hold the other harmless from and against any and all claims, loss, liability, damage or expenses (including reasonable attorneys' fees) suffered or incurred by the other party as a result of a claim brought by a person or entity engaged or claiming to be engaged as a finder, broker or agent by the indemnifying party.

8.15 Survival of Covenants. Any covenant, term or provision of this Agreement which, in order to be effective, must survive the termination of this Agreement, shall survive any such termination.

8.16 Estoppel Certificate. Manager, the Enterprise and the Tribe agree to furnish to any other party, from time to time upon request, an estoppel certificate in such reasonable form as the requesting party may request stating whether there have been any defaults under this Agreement known to the party furnishing the estoppel certificate and such other information relating to the Facility as may be reasonably requested.

8.17 Periods of Time. Whenever any determination is to be made or action is to be taken on a date specified in this Agreement, if such date shall fall on a Saturday, Sunday or legal holiday under the laws of the Tribe, federal government, or the State of California, then in such event said date shall be extended to the next day which is not a Saturday, Sunday or legal holiday.

8.18 <u>Exhibits.</u> All exhibits attached hereto are incorporated herein by reference and made a part hereof as if fully rewritten or reproduced herein.

8.19 <u>Successors, Assigns, and Subcontracting.</u> The benefits and obligations of this Agreement shall inure to and be binding upon the parties hereto and their respective successors and assigns. Manager shall have the right to assign its rights under this Agreement to one or more directly or indirectly wholly owned subsidiaries of Trump Hotels & Casino Resorts, Inc., or its successor. The Enterprise's consent shall be required for the assignment or subcontracting by Manager of its rights, interests or obligations as Manager hereunder to any person or entity other than an Affiliate of Manager, or any successor corporation to Manager, provided that any such assignee or subcontractor agrees to be bound by the terms and conditions of this Agreement, and the Enterprise shall consent to any such assignee or subcontractor provided that such assignee or subcontractor has, in the discretion of the Enterprise, the competency and financial capability to perform as required by this Agreement. The acquisition of Manager or its parent company by a party other than an Affiliate of Manager, or its successor corporation, shall not constitute an assignment of this Agreement by Manager and this Agreement shall remain in full force and effect between the Tribe, the Enterprise and Manager, subject only to Legal Requirements. In all respects, any assignment or subcontracting permitted pursuant to this Section 8.19 shall be subject to the notification requirements provided in Section 13.4 of this Agreement and any required approval by the NIGC.

8.20 <u>Permitted Assignment.</u> Any assignment of this Agreement permitted under the Agreement, to the extent mandated by the IGRA, shall be subject to approval by the Chairman of the NIGC or his authorized representative after a complete background investigation of the proposed assignee. The Tribe or Enterprise shall, without the consent of Manager but subject to approval by the Secretary of the Interior or the Chairman of the NIGC or his authorized representative, have the right to assign this Agreement and the assets of the Facility to an instrumentality of the Tribe or to a corporation wholly-owned by the-Tribe organized to conduct the business of the Enterprise for the Tribe that assumes all obligations herein. Any assignment by the Tribe shall not prejudice the rights of Manager under this Agreement. No assignment authorized hereunder shall be effective until all necessary government approvals have been obtained.

8.21 Time is of the Essence. Time is of the essence in the performance of this Agreement.

8.22 Confidential Information. The parties agree that any information received concerning any other party during the performance of this Agreement, regarding the parties' organization, financial matters, marketing plans, or other information of a proprietary nature (the "Confidential Information"), will be treated by both parties in full confidence and except as required to allow Manager, the Enterprise and the Tribe to perform their respective covenants and obligations hereunder, or in response to legal process or appropriate and necessary inquiry, and will not be revealed to any other persons, firms or organizations. This provision shall survive the termination of this Agreement for a period of two (2) years.

The obligations not to use or disclose the Confidential Information shall not apply to Confidential Information which (i) has been made previously available to the public by the Tribe, the Enterprise or Manager or becomes generally available to the public, unless the Confidential Information being made available to the public results in a breach of this Agreement; **(ii)** prior to disclosure to the Tribe, the Enterprise or Manager, was already rightfully in any such person's possession; or **(iii)** is obtained by the Tribe, the Enterprise or Manager from a third party who is lawfully in possession of such Confidential Information, and not in violation of any contractual, legal or fiduciary obligation to the Tribe, the Enterprise or Manager, with respect to such Confidential Information and who does not require the Tribe, the Enterprise or Manager to refrain from disclosing such Confidential Information to others.

8.23 Patron Dispute Resolution. Manager shall submit all patron disputes concerning play to the Tribal Gaming Authority pursuant to the Tribal Gaming Code, and the regulations promulgated thereunder.

8.24 Modification. Any change to or modification of this Agreement must be in writing signed by all parties hereto and shall be effective only upon approval by the Chairman of the NIGC, the date of signature of the parties notwithstanding.

SECTION 9
WARRANTIES

9.1 <u>**Noninterference in Tribal Affairs.**</u> Manager agrees not to interfere in or attempt to wrongfully influence the internal affairs or government decisions of the Tribal Council or the Enterprise by offering cash incentives, by making written or oral threats to the personal or financial status of any person, or by any other action, except for actions in the normal course of business of Manager that relate to the Facility. As of the date of this Agreement, the Tribe and the Enterprise acknowledge that Manager has not interfered or wrongfully interfered in the internal affairs of the Tribe and the Enterprise. For the purposes of this Section 9.1, if any such undue interference in Tribal affairs is alleged by the federally recognized Tribal government in writing and the NIGC finds that Manager has unduly interfered with the internal affairs of the Tribe government and has not taken sufficient action to cure and prevent such interference, that finding of interference shall be grounds for termination of the Agreement. Manager shall be entitled to immediate written notice and a complete copy of any such complaint to the NIGC.

9.2 <u>**Prohibition of Payments to Members of Tribal Government.**</u> Manager represents and warrants that no payments have been or will be made by Manager or Manager's Affiliates, to any Member of the Tribal Government, any Tribal official, any relative of a Member of Tribal Government or Tribal official, or any Tribal government employee for the purpose of obtaining any special privilege, gain, advantage or consideration.

9.3 <u>**Prohibition of Hiring Members of Tribal Government.**</u> No Member of the Tribal Government, Tribal official, or employee of the Tribal government may be employed at the Facility or Manager or its Affiliates without a written waiver of this Section 9.3 by the Tribe. For this purpose, the Tribe will identify all such persons to Manager in a writing and take reasonable steps to keep the list current; Manager shall not be held responsible if any person not on such written list is employed.

9.4 <u>**Prohibition of Financial Interest in Enterprise.**</u> No Member of the Tribal Government or relative of a Member of the Tribal Government shall have a direct or indirect financial interest in the

Enterprise greater than the interest of any other member of the Tribe. No Member of the Tribal Government or relative of a Member of the Tribal Government shall have a direct or indirect financial interest in Manager or Manager's Affiliates.

9.5 Definitions. As used in this Section 9, "Member of the Tribal Government" means any member of the Tribal Council, the Tribal Gaming Authority or any independent board or body created to oversee any aspect of Gaming and any Tribal court official; "Relative" means an individual residing in the same household who is related as a spouse, father, mother, son or daughter.

SECTION 10
TERMINATION

10.1 Voluntary Termination and Termination for Cause. This Agreement may be terminated pursuant to the provisions of Sections 3.4.4, 10.2, 10.3, 10.4, 10.5 and 10.6 and 10.10.

10.2 Voluntary Termination. This Agreement may be terminated upon the mutual written consent and approval of the parties.

10.3 Termination for Cause. Either the Tribe or the Enterprise may terminate this Agreement if Manager commits or allows to be committed any Material Breach of this Agreement, and Manager may terminate this Agreement if either the Tribe or the Enterprise commits or allows to be committed any Material Breach of this Agreement,. A Material Breach of this Agreement means a failure of any party to perform any material duty or obligation on its part for any thirty (30) consecutive days after notice, and shall include, but not be limited to, those events identified as a Material Breach in Section 13.5 of this Agreement. Any action taken or the adoption of any statute or code that taxes, materially prejudices or materially adversely affects or imposes additional costs or burdens on Manager's rights or duties under this Agreement shall be a Material Breach of this Agreement by the Tribe. No party may terminate this Agreement on grounds of Material Breach unless it has provided written notice to the other parties of its intention to declare a default and to terminate this Agreement and the defaulting party thereafter fails to cure or take steps to substantially cure the default within sixty (60) days following receipt of such notice. During the period specified in the notice to terminate, any party may submit the matter to arbitration under the dispute resolution provisions of this Agreement at Section 16. The discontinuance or correction of a Material Breach shall constitute a cure thereof.

An election to pursue damages or to pursue specific performance of this Agreement or other equitable remedies while this Agreement remains in effect pursuant to the provisions of Sections 10.7 or 10.8 shall not preclude the injured party from providing notice of termination pursuant to this Section 10.3. Neither shall termination preclude a suit for damages.

10.4 <u>Involuntary Termination Due to Changes in Legal Requirements.</u> It is the understanding and intention of the parties that the establishment and operation of the Facility shall conform to and comply with all Legal Requirements. If during the term of this Agreement, the Facility or any material aspect of Gaming is determined by the Congress of the United States, the Department of the Interior of the United States of America, the NIGC, or the final judgment of a court of competent jurisdiction to be unlawful under federal law, the obligations of the parties hereto shall cease, and this Agreement shall be of no further force and effect; provided that:

Manager shall have the rights described in Section 3.4 of this Agreement; Manager, the Tribe and the Enterprise shall retain all money previously paid to them pursuant to Section 5 of this Agreement; funds of the Enterprise in any Enterprise account shall be paid and distributed as provided in Section 5 of this Agreement;

The Enterprise shall retain its interest in the title (and any lease) to all Facility assets, including all fixtures, supplies and equipment, subject to any requirements of financing arrangements.

10.5 <u>Manager's Right to Terminate Agreement.</u> Manager may terminate this Agreement by written notice effective upon receipt if:

Any Tribal, State or Federal authority where approval is required fails to approve this Agreement or otherwise objects to the performance by Manager of any obligation imposed on it under this Agreement. Manager has been notified by any Federal regulatory agency that the performance by it of any obligation imposed by this Agreement will jeopardize the retention of any license, or approvals granted thereunder, held by Manager or any of its Affiliates in other jurisdiction, and the Tribe or the Enterprise refuses to allow Manager to immediately rectify any such complaint. Manager has reason to believe that the performance by it, by the Enterprise or by the Tribe of any obligation imposed under this Agreement may reasonably be expected to result in the breach of any Legal Requirement and the parties have been unable to agree upon waiver of such performance within ten (10) days written notice by Manager.

Through its own actions, the Tribe or the Enterprise fails to make any payment to Manager when due within the time specified in this Agreement and a grace period of thirty (30) days.

10.6 <u>**Tribe's and Enterprise's Right to Terminate Agreement.**</u> In addition to the suspension of Manager pursuant to Section 10.9 herein, the Tribe or the Enterprise may terminate this Agreement by written notice effective upon receipt if any Federal or State authority, where approval is required, fails to approve this Agreement or otherwise objects to the performance by Manager of any obligation imposed on it under this Agreement and Manager has not cured the circumstance giving rise to the failure to approve or the objection to performance within thirty (30) days.

The Tribe has reason to believe that the performance by it, the Enterprise or Manager of any obligation imposed under this Agreement may reasonably be expected to result in the breach of any Legal Requirement (other than a Legal Requirement imposed or created by the Tribe or any agency thereof) and the parties have been unable to agree upon waiver of such performance within ten (10) days of written notice given by the Tribe. Manager fails to make any payment to the Tribe or the Enterprise when due, including but not limited to any Minimum Guaranteed Monthly Payment to the Tribe within the time specified in this Agreement and a grace period of thirty (30) days. Manager has had its license withdrawn because Manager, or a director or officer of Manager, has been convicted of a criminal felony or misdemeanor offense in the performance of Manager duties hereunder, or where Manager has failed to disclose any such conviction to the Tribal Gaming Authority promptly upon Manager receiving notice thereof; provided, however, the Tribe or the Enterprise may not terminate this Agreement based on a director or officer's conviction where Manager terminates such individual within ten (10) days after receiving notice of the conviction.

10.7 <u>**Consequences of Manager's Breach.**</u> In the event of the termination of this Agreement by the Tribe or the Enterprise for cause under Section 10.3, Manager shall not, prospectively from the date of termination, except as provided in Section 10.3, have the right to its Management Fee from the Facility, but such termination shall not affect Manager's rights relating to recoupment and reimbursement of monies owed to Manager and/or guaranteed by Manager and/or Manager's Affiliates (to the extent Manager or Manager's

Affiliate has paid under such guarantee) under this Agreement, the Financing Agreements, the Note, the Manager Guaranty or any other agreements entered pursuant hereto, including a Shortfall Amount, and such right of recoupment and reimbursement shall survive any termination of this Agreement. Any Net Revenues accruing through the date of termination shall be distributed in accordance with Section 5 of this Agreement. Manager, the Tribe and the Enterprise acknowledge and agree that termination of this Agreement may not be a sufficient or appropriate remedy for breach by Manager, and further agree that pursuant to the other provisions of this Agreement, including, but not limited to, Section 16, the Tribe or the Enterprise shall, upon breach of this Agreement by Manager, have the right to pursue such remedies (in addition to termination) at law or equity as it determines are best able to compensate it for such breach. Manager specifically acknowledges and agrees that there may be irreparable harm to the Tribe or the Enterprise and that damages will be difficult to determine if Manager commits a Material Breach, and Manager therefore further acknowledges that an injunction and/or other equitable relief may be an appropriate remedy for any such breach. In any event, the Tribe shall have the right to all payments due to the Tribe accruing until the date of termination.

   10.8 <u>Consequences of Tribe's Breach.</u> In the event of termination of this Agreement by Manager for cause under Section 10.3, Manager shall not be required to perform any further services under this Agreement and the Enterprise shall indemnify and hold Manager harmless against all liabilities of any nature whatsoever relating to the Facility, but only insofar as these liabilities result from acts within the control of the Tribe or the Enterprise or their respective agents or created by the termination of this Agreement. Manager, the Tribe and the Enterprise acknowledge and agree that termination of this Agreement may not be a sufficient or appropriate remedy for breach by the Tribe or the Enterprise, and further agree that pursuant to the other provisions of this Agreement, including but not necessarily limited to, Section 16, Manager shall, upon breach of this Agreement by the Tribe or the Enterprise, have the right to pursue such remedies (in addition to termination) at law or equity as it determines are best able to compensate it for such breach, including, without limitation, specifically actions to require payment of the Management Fee pursuant to Section 5 for a term equal to the then remaining term of this Agreement at the percentage of Net Revenues specified in Section 5. The Tribe and the Enterprise specifically acknowledge and agree that there may be irreparable harm to Manager and that damages will be difficult to determine if the Tribe or the Enterprise commits a material breach, and the Tribe and the Enterprise therefore further acknowledge that an injunction and/or other equitable relief may be an appropriate remedy for any such breach.

10.9 <u>Suspension of Manager for Cause; Notice and Opportunity to Cure.</u> In the event of any breach of this Agreement by Manager involving a violation by Manager of any Legal Requirements, the Enterprise may immediately suspend the right and authority of Manager to manage the Facility unless and until such breach is remedied or cured by Manager. The Enterprise will give Manager notice of any alleged violation of the Tribal Gaming Code by Manager and twenty (20) days opportunity to cure before the Tribal Gaming Authority may take any action other than suspension of the Manager based on such alleged violation.

10.10 <u>Enterprise's Buy-Out Option.</u> The Enterprise shall have the right to If the Enterprise fails to satisfy any of the above conditions on or before the dates specified above, then this option and any attempted exercise thereof shall be null and void and of no further force or effect, and this Agreement shall continue in full force and effect according to its terms.

SECTION 11
CONCLUSION OF THE MANAGEMENT TERM

11.1 <u>Conclusion of the Management Term.</u> Upon the conclusion or the termination of this Agreement, Manager shall have the following rights and obligations:

11.2 <u>Transition.</u> Manager shall take reasonable steps for the orderly transition of management of the Facility to the Tribe, the Enterprise or its designee pursuant to a transition plan as described in Section 17 of this Agreement.

11.3 <u>Undistributed Net Revenues.</u> If the Facility has accrued Net Revenues which have not been distributed under Section 5 of this Agreement, Manager shall receive that Management Fee equal to that Management Fee it would have received had the distribution occurred during the term of the Management Agreement (including any Shortfall Amount, but upon termination at the conclusion of the Term, only to the extent of Excess Funds).

SECTION 12
CONSENTS AND APPROVALS

12.1 <u>Tribal.</u> Where approval or consent or other action of the Tribe is required, such approval shall mean the written approval of the Tribal Council evidenced by a resolution thereof, certified by a Tribal official as having been duly adopted, or such other person or entity designated by resolution of the Tribal Council. Any such approval, consent or action shall not be unreasonably withheld or delayed; provided that the foregoing does not apply where a specific provision of this Agreement allows the Tribe an absolute right to deny approval or consent or withhold action.

12.2 <u>Manager.</u> Where approval or consent or other action of Manager is required, such approval shall mean the written approval of an officer of Manager. Any such approval, consent or other action shall not be unreasonably withheld or delayed.

SECTION 13
DISCLOSURES

13.1 <u>Shareholders and Directors.</u> Manager warrants that on the date of this Agreement its Affiliates, shareholders, directors and officers are those listed on Exhibit G.

13.2 <u>Warranties.</u> Manager further warrants and represents as follows: no person or entity has any beneficial ownership interest in Manager other than as set forth herein; no officer, director or owner of ten (10%) percent or more of the stock of Manager has been arrested, indicted for, convicted of, or pleaded *nolo contendere* to any felony or any gaming offense, or had any association with individuals or entities known to be connected with organized crime; and no person or entity listed on Exhibit G to this Agreement, including any officers and directors of Manager, has been arrested, indicted for, convicted of, or pleaded nolo contendere to any felony or any gaming offense, or had any association with individuals or entities known to be connected with organized crime.

13.3 <u>Criminal and Credit Investigation.</u> Manager agrees that all of its shareholders, directors and officers (whether or not involved in the Facility), shall: consent to background investigations to be conducted by the Tribe, the State of California, the Federal Bureau of Investigation (the "FBI") or any other law enforcement authority to the extent required by the IGRA and the Compact; be subject to licensing requirements in accordance with Tribal law and this Agreement; consent to a background, criminal and credit investigation to be conducted by or for the NIGC, if required; consent to a financial and credit investigation to be conducted by a credit reporting or investigation agency at the request of the Tribe; cooperate fully with such investigations; and disclose any information requested by the Tribe which would facilitate the background and financial investigation.

Any materially false or deceptive disclosures or failure to cooperate fully with such investigations by an employee of Manager or an employee of the Tribe shall result in the immediate dismissal of such employee. The results of any such investigation may be disclosed by the Tribe to federal officials and to such other regulatory authorities as required by law.

13.4 Disclosure Amendments. The Tribe and Enterprise acknowledge that Manager is wholly owned by a publicly traded company, and that Manager's Affiliates, shareholders, directors and officers may change from time to time without the prior approval of the Tribe or the Enterprise. Manager agrees that whenever there is any material change in the information disclosed pursuant to this Section 13 it shall notify the Tribe of such change not later than ten (10) days following the change or within ten (10) days after it becomes aware of such change, whichever is later. In the event the change relates to information provided or required to be provided to the NIGC pursuant to 25 C.F.R 537.1, Manager shall notify the NIGC in sufficient time to permit the NIGC to complete its background investigation by the time the individual is to assume management responsibility for the gaming operation, and within ten (10) days of any proposed change in financial interest. All of the warranties and agreements contained in this Section 13 shall apply to any person or entity who would be listed in this Section 13 as a result of such changes.

13.5 Breach of Manager's Warranties and Agreements. The material breach of any warranty or agreement of Manager contained in this Section 13 shall be grounds for immediate termination of this Agreement; provided that (i) if a breach of the warranty contained in clause (ii) of Section 13.2 is discovered, and such breach was not disclosed by any background check conducted by the FBI as part of the BIA or other federal approval of this Agreement, or was discovered by the FBI investigation but all officers and directors of Manager sign sworn affidavits that they had no knowledge of such breach, then Manager shall have thirty (30) days after notice from the Tribe to terminate the interest of the offending person or entity and, if such termination takes place, this Agreement shall remain in full force and effect; and (ii) if a breach relates to a failure to update changes in financial position or additional gaming related activities, then Manager shall have ten (10) days after notice from the Tribe to cure such default prior to termination.

SECTION 14
RECORDATION

At the option of the Lender, Manager, the Enterprise or the Tribe, any security agreement related to the Financing Agreements may be recorded in any public records. Where such recordation is desired in any relevant recording office maintained by the Tribe, and/or in the public records of the BIA, the Tribe or the Enterprise will accomplish such recordation upon the request of the Lender or Manager, as the case may be. No such recordation shall be deemed to waive the Tribe's or the Enterprise's sovereign immunity.

SECTION 15
NO LIEN, LEASE OR JOINT VENTURE

The parties agree and expressly warrant that neither the Management Agreement nor any exhibit thereto is a mortgage or lease and, consequently, does not convey any present interest whatsoever in the Facility or the Property, nor any proprietary interest in the Facility itself. The parties further agree and acknowledge that it is not their intent, and that this Agreement shall not be construed, to create a joint venture between the Tribe or the Enterprise and Manager; rather, Manager shall be deemed to be an independent contractor for all purposes hereunder.

SECTION 16
DISPUTE RESOLUTION

16.1 General. The parties agree that binding arbitration shall be the remedy for all disputes, controversies and claims arising out of this Agreement, any documents referenced by any of this Agreement, any agreements collateral thereto, or any notice of termination thereof, including without limitation, any dispute, controversy or claim arising out of any of these agreements; provided, however, that actions or decisions by the Tribe that constitute the exercise of its sovereign governmental powers shall not be subject to arbitration, including decisions or actions by the Tribal Gaming Authority regarding the issuance or denial of licenses, and actions by the Tribal Council regarding the approval of budgets or the enactment of ordinances relating to Gaming. The Tribe acknowledges, however, that while the exercise of its governmental powers in a manner contrary to a provision of this Agreement may not be avoided through arbitration, Manager may compel arbitration pursuant to this Section 16 to redress any injury suffered by Manager as a result of such exercise. The parties intend that such arbitration shall provide final and binding resolution of any dispute, controversy or claim, and that action in any other forum shall be brought only if necessary to compel arbitration, or to enforce an arbitration award or order. All initial arbitration or judicial proceedings shall be instituted within twelve (12) months after the claim accrues or shall be forever barred.

Each party agrees that it will use its best efforts to negotiate an amicable resolution of any dispute between Manager and the Enterprise or the Tribe arising from this Agreement. If the Tribe or the Enterprise and Manager are unable to negotiate an amicable resolution of a dispute within fourteen (14) days from the date of notice of the dispute pursuant to the notice section of this Agreement, or such other period as the parties mutually agree in writing, either party may refer the matter to arbitration as provided herein.

16.2 Initiation of Arbitration and Selection of Arbitrators. Arbitration shall be initiated by written notice by one party to the other pursuant to the notice section of this Agreement, and the Commercial Arbitration Rules of the American Arbitration Association shall thereafter apply. The arbitrators shall have the power to grant equitable and injunctive relief and specific performance as provided in this Agreement. If necessary, orders to compel arbitration or enforce an arbitration award may be sought before the United States District Court for the Central District of California and any federal court having appellate jurisdiction over said court. If the United States District Court for the Central District of California finds that it lacks jurisdiction, the Tribe and the Enterprise consent to be sued in the California State Court system. This consent to California State Court jurisdiction shall only apply if Manager exercises reasonable efforts to argue for the jurisdiction of the federal court over said matter. The arbitrator shall be a licensed attorney, knowledgeable in federal Indian law and selected pursuant to the Commercial Arbitration Rules of the American Arbitration Association.

Unless the parties agree upon the appointment of a single arbitrator, a panel of arbitrators consisting of three (3) members shall be appointed. One (1) member shall be appointed by the Tribe and one (1) member shall be appointed by Manager within ten (10) working days' time following the giving of notice submitting a dispute to arbitration. The third member shall be selected by agreement of the other two (2) members. In the event the two (2) members cannot agree upon the third arbitrator within fifteen (15) working days' time, then the third arbitrator shall be chosen by the American Arbitration Association. Alternatively, the parties may, prior to any dispute, agree in advance upon a panel of arbitrators or a single arbitrator to which any dispute that may arise shall be submitted for resolution pursuant to this Section 16.2. Choice of Law. In determining any matter the arbitrators shall apply the terms of this Agreement, without adding to, modifying or changing the terms in any respect, and shall apply federal and applicable State law. Place of Hearing. All arbitration hearings shall be held at a place designated by the arbitrators in Los Angeles or Los Angeles County, California.

Confidentiality. The parties and the arbitrators shall maintain strict confidentiality with respect to arbitration.

16.3 Limited Waiver of Sovereign Immunity. The Tribe and the Enterprise expressly and irrevocably waives its respective immunity from suit as provided for and limited by this Section. This waiver is limited to the Tribe's and the Enterprise's consent to all arbitration proceedings, and actions to compel arbitration and to enforce any awards or orders issuing from such arbitration proceedings which are sought solely in United States District Court for the Central District of California and any federal court having appellate jurisdiction over said court, provided that if the United States District Court for the Central District of California finds that it lacks jurisdiction, the Tribe and the Enterprise consent to such actions in the California State Court system. This consent to California State Court jurisdiction shall only apply if Manager exercises reasonable efforts to argue for the jurisdiction of the federal court over said matter. The arbitrators shall not have the power to award punitive damages. <u>Time Period.</u> The waiver granted herein shall commence as of the Date of this Agreement and shall continue for following expiration, termination or cancellation of this Agreement, but shall remain effective for the duration of any arbitration, litigation or dispute resolution proceedings then pending, all appeals therefrom, and except as limited by this Section, to the full satisfaction of any awards or judgments which may issue from such proceedings, provided that an action to collect such judgments has been filed within one year of the date of the final judgment. <u>Recipient of Waiver.</u> This limited waiver is granted only to Manager and not to any other individual or entity. <u>Limitations of Actions.</u> This limited waiver is specifically limited to the following actions and judicial remedies: The enforcement of an arbitrator's award of money damages provided that the waiver does not extend beyond the assets specified in Subsection (iii) below. No arbitrator or court shall have any authority or jurisdiction to order execution against any assets or revenues of the Tribe or the Enterprise except as provided in this Section or to award any punitive damages against the Tribe or the Enterprise. An action to compel or enforce arbitration or arbitration awards or orders. Damages awarded against the Tribe or the Enterprise shall be satisfied solely from the distributable share of Net Revenues of the Tribe from the Facility, the tangible assets of the Facility and the business of the Enterprise, provided, however, that this limited waiver of sovereign immunity shall terminate with respect to the collection of any Net Revenues transferred from the accounts of the Enterprise to the Tribe or the Tribe's separate bank account in the normal course of business in accordance with this Agreement. In no instance shall any enforcement of any kind whatsoever be allowed against any assets of the Tribe other than those specified in this subsection.

SECTION 17
NEGOTIATE NEW AGREEMENT

17.1 <u>Intent to Negotiate New Agreement.</u> On or before thirty (30) days after the Enterprise shall give Manager notice of its intent regarding its willingness to enter into negotiations for a new Management Agreement to be effective upon the conclusion of this Agreement.

17.2 <u>Transition Plan.</u> If the Enterprise and Manager are unable to agree to the terms of a new agreement or if the Enterprise decides not to enter into negotiations for a new agreement, then the Enterprise and Manager shall agree upon a transition plan within thirty (30) days' notice from the Enterprise of its intention not to negotiate a new Management Agreement, which plan shall be sufficient to allow the Tribe and/or the Enterprise to operate the Facility and provide for the orderly transition of the management of the Facility.

SECTION 18
ENTIRE AGREEMENT

This Agreement, including the Schedules and Exhibits referred to herein, constitutes the entire understanding and agreement of the parties hereto and supersedes all other prior agreements and understandings, written or oral, between the parties. The parties acknowledge that the Tribe is entering into a Gaming Facility Construction and Development Agreement and a Trademark License Agreement with affiliates of Manager contemporaneously with this Agreement.

SECTION 19
REQUIRED AMENDMENT

Each of the parties agrees to execute, deliver and, if necessary, record any and all additional instruments, certifications, amendments, modifications and other documents as may be required by the United States Department of the Interior, BIA, the NIGC, the office of the Field Solicitor, or any applicable statute, rule or regulation in order to effectuate, complete, perfect, continue or preserve the respective rights, obligations, liens and interests of the parties hereto to the fullest extent permitted by law; provided, that any such additional instrument, certification, amendment, modification or other document shall not materially change the respective rights, remedies or obligations of the Tribe, the Enterprise or Manager under this Agreement or any other agreement or document related hereto.

SECTION 20
PREPARATION OF AGREEMENT

This Agreement was drafted and entered into after careful review and upon the advice of competent counsel; it shall not be construed more strongly for or against any party.

Following is the original signature page:

SECTION 21
STANDARD OF REASONABLENESS

Unless specifically provided otherwise, all provisions of this Agreement and all collateral agreements shall be governed by a standard of reasonableness.

SECTION 22
EXECUTION

This Agreement may be executed in four counterparts, one to be retained by each of the Tribe and the Enterprise, and two to be retained by Manager. Each of the four originals is equally valid. This Agreement shall be deemed "executed" and shall be binding upon both parties when properly executed and approved by the Chairman of the NIGC.

IN WITNESS WHEREOF, the parties hereto have executed this Agreement on the day and year first above written.

THCR MANAGEMENT SERVICES, LLC

By: _____
Donald J. Trump, President

TWENTY-NINE PALMS BAND OF LUISENO
MISSION INDIANS OF CALIFORNIA

By: _____
Dean Mike, Chairperson

TWENTY-NINE PALMS
ENTERPRISES CORPORATION

By: _____
Dean Mike, President

By: _____
Gene Gambale, Secretary

Approved by:
_____
Montie R. Deer, Chairman
National Indian Gaming Commission

April 15 - 2002
Date

CPSIA information can be obtained
at www.ICGtesting.com
Printed in the USA
LVOW08*1817050817
543915LV00010B/184/P